"Catholic catechists need basic tools to hand on the symbols of faith. With *Basics of the Catholic Faith*, the Colemans give us, in plain terms, a wealth of straightforward information about the Catholic faith presented in a manner designed to touch the heart. The main words to describe this book are 'simple' and 'useful.' Every catechist can remember multiple occasions when they have wished they had such a tool at hand—and now they do!"

Dennis M. Doyle
Professor of Religious Studies,
University of Dayton

"Here is an intriguing mix: an entertaining, informative spirituality book interspersed with a sort of 'pop quiz' update on some facts and practices that we Catholics happily take for granted. Replete with sayings, reading, excerpts, insights, prayers, poetry, *Basics of the Catholic Faith* is a way of getting reacquainted with things we thought we knew and had forgotten about. Peek into these nooks and crannies of the Church while walking with the Colemans down Catholicism's 2,000 year-long broad main aisle."

Arthur Jones, Editor-at-large
National Catholic Reporter

"This is a most unusual book. It answers basic questions about Catholic Christianity with sound information from tradition, history, and contemporary studies. The authors provide both overview and review of essentials and popular traditions for the curious, the inquirer, and the faithful. A detailed Table of Contents and Appendix guide the reader's search for specific issues and information."

Dr. Greg Dues
Author of *Catholic Customs and Traditions*
and *Enjoying God and Teaching Creatively*

"The veteran Coleman writing team of father Bill and mother Patty—now joined by their daughter Lisa—offer here an easy-to-read synthesis of the Catholic faith, its traditions, special language, worship, commitment to Jesus and the Father, the saints, and the Church's way of prayer. Here is a simple presentation of the basics, which anyone who identifies as being Catholic will find beneficial as a quick source for reliable information."

Bill Holub
Long-time Catholic publishing executive

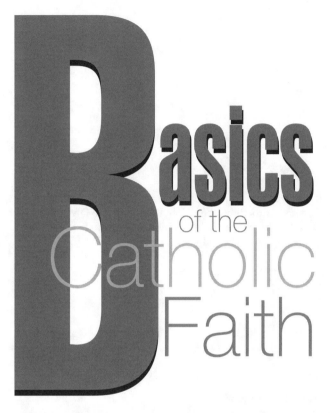

Basics of the Catholic Faith

Bill, Patty and Lisa Coleman

TWENTY-THIRD PUBLICATIONS
BAYARD Mystic, CT 06355

Twenty-Third Publications
A Division of Bayard
185 Willow Street
P.O. Box 180
Mystic, CT 06355
(860) 536-2611
(800) 321-0411
www.twentythirdpublications.com

ISBN:1-58595-109-9
Library of Congress Catalog Card Number: 00-133677
Printed in the U.S.A.

Dedication

to Ethel and Athena

Contents

Focus on the Church 41

Focus on Sacraments & Public Prayer 67

A Word
of Welcome

Two thousand years ago, Jesus of Nazareth opened his arms
to welcome all who came to him. Most were simple people
burdened with all the troubles and confusion life inevitably
brings. Some were educated, others not; some were rich,
some poor; some successful, others not; some in good
health, others ill; some rigidly confident in their Jewish
observance of the Law, others plagued with doubts; some
with well loved hearts, others whose hearts knew only lone-
liness and desolation. Yet, all found in Jesus the answer to
their questions and the healing of their hearts.

Twenty centuries later, we make that same journey to Jesus
for much the same reasons. We, too, are burdened with the
trouble and confusion life brings. We, too, have come to listen, but more than that, to embrace Jesus' way, to become his
friends, his followers.

We can begin by pondering one of Jesus' stories (Matthew
13:31–32). It is short, only a few lines long, but ever so
important for it speaks about God's power and presence in
our lives and in the world around us. Jesus used the symbol

of the mustard seed because he understood that people were wondering where God was in the midst of their confused and troubled lives. He said that God's reign, what the people of his time called the kingdom of God, was like a tiny mustard seed, the smallest of all the seeds. It would grow slowly, almost imperceptibly, unnoticed by busy people, until it became the greatest of all the bushes, large enough for the birds of the air to nestle in its branches.

This kingdom of God is still growing and we who come to Jesus today are a part of it. We are like "mustard seed people," you and I. Every good deed we do, every advance we make toward integrity, every time we reach out to heal our broken world, God's kingdom grows.

Like the mustard plant's branches, we are never alone. We are tied together like the parts of one living plant. We share a common life. Saint Paul says we are one body. Other parts of the Bible speak of us as the children of God, one family under God's loving protection.

We may have entered that mustard seed family by becoming members of the Catholic church in infancy or we may have found it in other Christian churches. Others have found it in their own special ways but to us this Catholic family with its traditions and heritage, its compassion and tenderness, its organization and sacraments is our home. Through it we become disciples of Christ.

Basics of the Catholic Faith is about following Jesus in this family—about its traditions, its special language, its worship, its commitment to Jesus and his Father, its heroes and heroines, and its way of prayer. We are proud to be members not because this makes us better than other people but because the Catholic church is our home, our own family, our way of following Jesus.

Jesus at the Center

The center of all Christianity is Jesus of Nazareth, the Christ, the Son of God. For twenty centuries, his followers have thought about him, dreamed about him, talked about him, prayed to him, and then written about their insights in many forms. This first section of *Basics of the Catholic Faith* shares with you some of those insights.

Coming to know and love Jesus is more than an intellectual pursuit, more than amassing information. It is a mystical and emotional experience as well, much like a boy who falls in love with the girl who lives next door. For years he had known about her, the color of her hair, her height, her family background, her friends, her education, her job, even her likes and dislikes. Yet, all of this was only knowledge, the kind of information he had about many other friends. Then, suddenly his eyes were opened and he was able to go beyond his knowing about her to love her, a love which transformed his knowledge and made it so profound it turned his whole life upside down.

The short readings that follow will introduce you to a variety of visions of Jesus. Some are theological, some mystical and poetic. Some are as ancient as the New Testament, some as contemporary as today. Our prayer is that one of them will so strike you that your eyes will be opened to see beyond your present knowledge of Jesus to love him—and perhaps to turn your life upside down.

One Solitary Life

We don't know who wrote this short piece or when. It was probably composed about two hundred years ago by a believer who was deeply affected by the life of Jesus.

Here is a man who was born of Jewish parents, the child of a peasant woman. He never wrote a book. He never held an office. He never owned a home. He never had a family. He never went to college. He never set foot inside a big city. He never traveled 200 miles from the place where he was born.

He never did one thing that usually accompanies greatness. He had no credentials but himself.

While still a young man he saw the tide of popular opinion turn against him. His friends ran away. One of them denied he knew him. He was turned over to his enemies and went through a mockery of a trial; then he was nailed to a cross between two thieves. His executioners gambled for the only piece of property he had on earth—his coat. When he was dead he was taken down (from the cross) and laid in a borrowed grave through the pity of a friend.

Nineteen wide centuries have come and gone and he is still the centerpiece of the human race and the leader of the column of progress. I am far within the mark when I say that all the armies that ever marched, and all the navies that were ever built have not affected the life of man upon earth as powerfully as has that One Solitary Life.

■ ANONYMOUS

The Mystery of Jesus

For three centuries after the resurrection of Jesus, Christians quietly accepted that he was both God and human. They made no effort to explain the mystery. Like so many things in life, this mystery was just there. By the year 300 A.D. some theologians tried to explain away the mystery and say Jesus was indeed a wonderful human being and very much like God but nothing more. A great controversy erupted involving bishops, theologians, and politicians on both sides of the question. The first worldwide meeting of the church's bishops met in 325 A.D. in Nicaea, a little town in what is now Turkey, and set the matter to rest. This is the part of their statement of faith which deals with Jesus. It is called the Nicene Creed which we still say together at Sunday Mass.

We believe in one Lord, Jesus Christ,
    the only Son of God,
eternally begotten of the Father,
God from God, Light from Light,
true God from true God,
begotten, not made, one in Being with the Father.
Through him all things were made.
For us and for our salvation
he came down from heaven:
by the power of the Holy Spirit
he was born of the Virgin Mary, and became man.
For our sake he was crucified under Pontius Pilate;
he suffered, died, and was buried.
On the third day he rose again
    in fulfillment of the Scriptures;
he ascended into heaven
    and is seated at the right hand
    of the Father.
He will come again in glory to judge
    the living and the dead,
    and his kingdom will have no end.

■ THE NICENE CREED

The Sign of the Cross

Many people find the words of the Nicene Creed abstract and hard to understand. But there is a simpler statement of faith in Jesus' divinity. We call it the Sign of the Cross. In this short creed we profess our faith in three profound mysteries which are the bedrock of all Christian belief: the Trinity, the divinity of Jesus, and the saving power of his death on the cross.

In the name *(Notice this is singular for there is only one God.)*

of the Father, and of the Son, and of the Holy Spirit *(Notice the equality among the three names which tell us there are three persons, for only persons have names.)*

Amen *(We affirm our belief in these profound mysteries by saying "Yes, so be it," Amen.)*

We make the sign of the cross on our bodies to remember, "he suffered under Pontius Pilate, was crucified, died, and was buried. On the third day he rose from the dead."

Why Jesus?

Why did God send Jesus? Jesus himself answered this question quite simply, "I came that they may have life, and have it abundantly." (John 10:10)

For centuries theologians and mystics have meditated on these words, trying to understand this abundant life that Jesus came to give. From their writings we can distill four important truths about the purpose of Jesus' life.

1. Because Jesus became our brother, "like us in all things except sin" (Hebrews 4:15), we can be a part of God's own family. We can experience a oneness with the Father as our brother, Jesus, did.

2. The presence of Jesus among us teaches us the intensity of God's love for all humanity.

3. By observing the lifestyle of Jesus, we learn how to live as God wants us to live.

4. Because Jesus was one of us, his love of the Father and of us, his human brothers and sisters, forged a bridge between us and God. When we accept Jesus and his commandments to love God and our neighbor we are saved from lives of selfishness and sin.

What People Saw in Jesus

What did Peter see?
And Andrew, James, and John?
And Mary and the Magdalene?
And all the others who watched his
peasant's life unfold?

They saw a strong man
resolutely marching
to a drummer they did not hear.

They saw a man of tenderness
whose impassioned touch could heal
and whose words went straight
to the heart of things
unsettling like the fine point of a surgeon's knife.

They saw a man who in time they knew
as more than a man,
the Anointed One
and, yes, the Son of God.

■ WILLIAM V. COLEMAN

Imitating Jesus

Abstract theological words, while filled with meaning, can so easily appear distant from our everyday lives. Here is a simple story of how one man discovered the meaning of the Incarnation.

Before integration, black people in the southern United States lived in one world, whites in another. I was white, highly educated, and at least middle-class but for some reason which still is not clear to me, I wanted to become friends with poor, uneducated, black people and somehow become a part of their community. I joined the NAACP and began attending their meetings which were held in a different little ramshackle church each week.

Every Sunday afternoon for months I never missed a meeting but somehow I remained an outsider. People were polite but never warm or friendly. Written on their faces were feelings of suspicion and mistrust. I was, after all, the only white person there.

One afternoon, the president invited me to give the opening prayer. As I prayed, I heard voices shouting from every corner of the church, "Amen," "Yes," "All right," "You tell 'em, brother." In that moment, I knew I was accepted. I had become one of the community. I was still white and they were black. I was still educated and most of them were not. I was still middle-class while they were poor. Yet, I was one of them. They called me "brother" and really meant it.

As I left the meeting I remembered the old catechism word, Incarnation. Without ceasing to be the all-wise and all-wonderful God, Jesus became our humble human brother. And yes, it seemed to me that we who follow Jesus must do as he did, become a part of the persecuted, poor and forgotten human community. For me, that is what Incarnation means.

■ WILLIAM V. COLEMAN

The Kingdom of God

Jesus inherited many expressions from the Jewish culture in which he lived and made them his own. No expression is more common and perhaps more misunderstood than this one.

The world around us is filled with evil—dishonesty, violence, hatred, oppression, disease, poverty, and natural calamity. Ancient Hebrews believed that all these evils were of a single piece and formed a kind of "kingdom of evil or darkness" in the world. They longed for a time when this kingdom would be overcome by their God, when light would conquer darkness. They prayed that his kingdom would come and come soon.

Gospel writers remembered that Jesus told his hearers to change their hearts for the kingdom of God was at hand. Jesus cured the sick, cast out demons, forgave sins, and announced the good news that the kingdom of God was breaking in on human history. His cures, his power over demons, his preaching were signs, signs that even the simplest could understand that indeed the kingdom of God was at hand.

Some Jewish people of Jesus' day, however, misunderstood the expression. They took the words literally and expected God to enter their history and set up a kingdom like the other kingdoms of the world. They believed that the kingdom of God would arrive momentarily and when it did they would be the kingdom's most important people.

Jesus insisted this kingdom which, like a mustard seed or leaven in the dough, will grow slowly, imperceptibly perhaps. For individuals, only heaven will bring the kind of justice and contentment promised by God. For society, however, the kingdom will continue to grow and quietly destroy evils until Jesus returns in glory at the end of this era.

All of this was in Jesus' mind when he taught us to pray, "Thy kingdom come." Then to be sure everyone understood just what the kingdom entailed, he added, "Thy will be done on earth as it is in heaven."

Theological Words about Jesus

Through the centuries theologians have invented words to express the mystery of Jesus. Many of them come from the fourth century when the whole church struggled to define its belief in the divinity of Jesus. Others are from the time of the Reformation when Catholic theologians tried to express their faith in clearer and more concise ways.

Here are some of the technical, theological words Christians use to discuss the mystery of Jesus.

Consubstantial—Jesus is God just as the Father is God. They share the same divine nature. It is not enough to say that he was the finest human who ever lived or even that he had a special relationship with God. Christians believe that Jesus is God.

Hypostatic union—once we come to believe that Jesus is God we must not forget that he is at the same time fully human with all that entails.

Nicene Creed—a formula of belief named from the First ecumenical council held in Nicaea in 325 A.D. It is the creed Catholics say at Sunday Mass and puts great emphasis on the divinity of Jesus.

Incarnation—the act by which God united himself to a human nature. This happened when the angel announced to Mary that she would be the mother of the Savior.

The Apostles' Creed—a very ancient baptismal creed with roots in the first century A.D. Catholics say it when they renew their baptismal promises at Easter.

Substance—a philosophical word meaning the essence of a thing and answers the question what is it? All three Persons in God have one substance for there is only one God.

Person—a philosophical word which names an intelligent substance and answers the question who is it? In the one

God (one substance) there are three distinct Persons, Father, Son, and Holy Spirit. Jesus is the Second Person, the Son.

Trinity—a philosophical word used by Christians for the three Persons in the one God.

Virgin Birth—God the Father was the father of Jesus. Mary, his mother, remained a virgin before and after the birth of Jesus.

Christology—theological study of Jesus, the Christ who lives in the church through the Holy Spirit.

Titles of Jesus

Early Christians used many different words to describe Jesus. Some of them throw light on what they believed him to be, fully human and yet fully divine.

Jesus of Nazareth—He came to us in human form, "born of a woman" as Saint Paul says, with clear historical origins and a connection with one town and one people.

Son of Mary—From the beginning Christians treasured the memory of his mother, Mary, and insisted that she had a prominent role in her son's saving work.

The Messiah—This word means "the anointed one." People were anointed to perform a special task such as to be a king or prophet or priest. Jews looked forward to one who was anointed by God to initiate his kingdom on earth.

Son of Man—In the Book of Daniel a figure appears called the Son of Man. The title was mystical and mysterious. Because early believers recognized in Jesus something beyond their understanding, this title seemed apt.

Son of God—From the beginning, Christians believed that Jesus was God's own Son. They did not know how to express this overpowering reality since they believed in only one God and so used this title "Son" to come as close as they dared to an incredible reality of faith.

Son of David—David was the most revered king of Israel. Everyone in Jesus' day expected that the messiah would be a descendant of David. This is why the church remembered that Jesus was born in Bethlehem, the town of David, a member of the house or family of the great king.

The Lord—This is one of the Jewish words used for God. Early believers said quite openly, "Jesus is Lord."

The Suffering Servant—The Prophet Isaiah called the nation of Israel the servant of the Lord, a servant called to suffer. Early believers saw that Jesus was a summation of all that was best in Israel and so suffered as the servant of his Father.

The Good Shepherd—a traditional title in the Hebrew Scriptures for God who shepherds his people, Israel. Jesus applied it to himself to emphasize his intimate knowledge and care for his followers.

Rabbi—a title of respect given to teachers of the Law and Traditions of Israel.

The Gospels

There is no better way to meet Jesus than through the gospel writers. Because these are ancient documents unlike any other we are likely to encounter, we may at first be a bit perplexed and have questions we need answered. Here are some questions people most often ask.

Q: What is a gospel?
A: The word "gospel" means good news. The good news is that God has come to dwell among us and to invite us to a new kind of life. In a sense, the good news is Jesus.

After Jesus' death and resurrection, four different people put this good news into writing. We call these writings the four gospels.

Q: Who wrote the gospels?

A: Tradition gives us the names of Matthew, Mark, Luke, and John. Today's scholars, however, are not absolutely sure who the writers were. Some speculate that the gospels were written and revised many times before the church accepted them in their present form.

Q: Who wrote Matthew's Gospel?

A: Tradition links the apostle Levi with Matthew. This version of the gospel was undoubtedly written for Jewish Christians, many of whom may have been profoundly depressed by the destruction of Jerusalem in 70 A.D. and wondered how their Jewish heritage fit into the new scheme of things. It may have been written first in Aramaic and later translated into Greek.

Q. Who wrote Mark's Gospel?

A: Tradition says that Mark was a member of the early church, a secretary to Saint Peter and wrote to a non-Jewish audience. Some scholars think his gospel was the first to be written and may have been used by both Matthew and Luke as a source and reference.

Q: Who was Luke?

A: Here tradition and scholars seem to agree. Luke never knew Jesus. He was a physician and companion of Saint Paul. He wrote both the gospel which bears his name, and the Acts of the Apostles. He emphasizes the concern of Jesus for the poor and powerless.

Q: Who was John?

A: The fourth gospel speaks of "the beloved disciple." Most think this is the apostle John who is believed to have lived until near the year 100 A.D. on the island of Patmos near present day Turkey. Some scholars believe that this gospel was written and revised until the end of the first century while others believe it was written fifty years earlier.

Q: Were there any other gospels?

A: Yes, there were but only these four were accepted by the church as the authentic word of God. Others, such as the Gospel of Thomas and the Gospel of Peter, were never incorporated into the Christian Bible. These other gospels are usually called "apocryphal" (which means of questionable authenticity).

Q: Do the apocryphal gospels add any information to what we already know about Jesus?

A: Most of the reliable stories in them were taken from the four gospels. Other stories are of doubtful value but are often found as the background for Christian art.

Q. What influence did the Dead Sea Scrolls have on the gospels?

A: The Dead Sea Scrolls, a collection of first-century writings found in southern Palestine in the 1940s and '50s, tell of a Jewish sect called the Essenes. They may have had some influence on John the Baptist but manifest little or no connection with Jesus or his followers. They are, however, very helpful in understanding the political and religious climate of the times.

Q: Why are the gospels so much alike?

A: The first three gospels have some common source. Earlier scholars believed it was no more than an oral tradition which served the church for thirty years or more after Jesus' resurrection. In a time when most read very little, if at all, people routinely memorized stories and creeds. Some scholars have suggested intricate theories of how one gospel was used as background for another. Still others have suggested that a now missing collection of Jesus' sayings provided the link. They call this missing document "The Q Document." We know that the first three gospels are similar and in many places parallel to one another. We do not know with certainty how they got that way.

Favorite Gospel Passages

There are, of course, a great many significant passages in the gospels. The following, taken from Matthew's Gospel, are some of the better known and often quoted.

Then Jesus was led up by the Spirit into the wilderness to be tempted by the devil. He fasted forty days and forty nights, and afterwards he was famished.   MATTHEW 4:1–2

From that time Jesus began to proclaim, "Repent, for the kingdom of heaven has come near."   MATTHEW 4:17

You are the salt of the earth; but if salt has lost its taste, how can its saltiness be restored? It is no longer good for anything, but is thrown out and trampled under foot.

MATTHEW 5:13

Do not store up for yourselves treasures on earth, where moth and rust consume and where thieves break in and steal; but store up for yourselves treasures in heaven, where neither moth nor rust consumes and where thieves do not break in and steal. For where your treasure is, there your heart will be also.   MATTHEW 6:19–21

No one can serve two masters; for a slave will either hate the one and love the other, or be devoted to the one and despise the other. You cannot serve God and wealth.

MATTHEW 6:24

Do not judge, so that you may not be judged.   MATTHEW 7:1

Ask, and it will be given you; search, and you will find; knock, and the door will be opened for you.   MATTHEW 7:7

In everything do to others as you would have them do to you; for this is the law and the prophets.   MATTHEW 7:12

Go and learn what this means, "I desire mercy, not sacrifice." For I have come to call not the righteous but sinners.

MATTHEW 9:13

Whoever welcomes you welcomes me, and whoever welcomes me welcomes the one who sent me.   MATTHEW 10:40

Come to me, all you that are weary and are carrying heavy burdens, and I will give you rest. Take my yoke upon you, and learn from me; for I am gentle and humble in heart, and you will find rest for your souls.   MATTHEW 11:28–29

Truly I tell you, unless you change and become like children, you will never enter the kingdom of heaven.

MATTHEW 18:3

Jesus said to him, "If you wish to be perfect, go, sell your possessions, and give the money to the poor, and you will have treasure in heaven; then come, follow me."

MATTHEW 19:21

It will not be so among you; but whoever wishes to be great among you must be your servant.   MATTHEW 20:26

And the king will answer them, "Truly I tell you, just as you did it to one of the least of these who are members of my family, you did it to me."   MATTHEW 25:40

While they were eating, Jesus took a loaf of bread, and after blessing it he broke it, gave it to the disciples, and said, "Take, eat; this is my body." Then he took a cup, and after giving thanks he gave it to them, saying, "Drink from it, all of you; for this is my blood of the covenant, which is poured out for many for the forgiveness of sins."   MATTHEW 26:26–28

Go therefore and make disciples of all nations, baptizing them in the name of the Father and of the Son and of the Holy Spirit, and teaching them to obey everything that I have commanded you. And remember, I am with you always, to the end of the age.   MATTHEW 28:19–20

Then Jesus cried again with a loud voice and breathed his last.   MATTHEW 27:50

He is not here; for he has been raised, as he said. Come, see the place where he lay.   MATTHEW 28:6

Gospel People

In this alphabetical list are some of the people you will meet as you read the four gospels:

Anna—an old woman who recognized Jesus as the messiah while he was still an infant.

Annas—the father-in-law of the high priest Caiaphas and a powerful Jewish leader.

Apostles—the twelve men Jesus chose to be his closest followers: Simon Peter, Andrew, James the greater, John, Philip, Bartholomew (also called Nathanael), Thomas, Matthew (also called Levi), James the less, Thaddaeus (also called Jude), Simon the Zealot, and Judas who betrayed Jesus.

Barabbas—a revolutionary held prisoner by the Romans who was released by Pilate in place of Jesus.

Caiaphas—the Jewish high priest who first suggested that Jesus be executed.

Cleopas—a disciple who met Jesus on the road to Emmaus.

Elizabeth—mother of John the Baptist and a cousin of Mary.

Gabriel—the angel who told Mary she was to be the mother of the messiah.

Herod—king of Judea at the time of Jesus' birth who ordered the slaughter of the innocent children of Bethlehem.

Herod Antipas—a ruler of part of Palestine after Herod's death. He beheaded John the Baptist.

Herodias—wife of Herod Antipas and mother of Salome who asked for John the Baptist's head upon a platter.

James—an apostle called by Jesus with his brother John while both were fishing. Also the name of another apostle who was the son of Alphaeus, sometimes called James the less. A third James was the leader of the early church in Jerusalem.

Joanna—one of the women whose contributions helped support Jesus and the apostles.

John—the apostle, brother of James, believed to be the author of the fourth gospel and some of the epistles.

John the Baptist—a cousin of Jesus and the man who prepared the Jewish people for his coming.

Joseph—the husband of Mary and foster-father of Jesus.

Joseph of Arimathea—follower of Jesus in whose tomb Jesus' body was laid.

Judas—the apostle who betrayed Jesus.

Lazarus—a friend whom Jesus raised from the dead, brother of Martha and Mary.

Luke—author of the third gospel, probably a companion of Saint Paul.

Mark—author of the second gospel and probably an early disciple of Jesus although not one of the Twelve.

Martha—sister of Mary and Lazarus and a friend of Jesus.

Mary—the mother of Jesus.

Mary Magdalene—an early follower of Jesus who was one of the first to see the risen Christ.

Mary, sister of Martha and Lazarus—and a friend of Jesus.

Mary, mother of James—present at Jesus' crucifixion.

Mary, the wife of Cleopas—also present at the crucifixion of Jesus.

Matthew—a tax collector turned apostle who wrote the first gospel. He is also called Levi.

Nicodemus—a leader of the Jewish people who came to visit Jesus at night so he would not be seen with him by others.

Peter—Peter or rock is the name Jesus gave to Simon, the most outspoken of the apostles and their natural leader, to remind him that he was to be the rock upon which others could rely. He is also called Cephas, another word meaning rock.

Pharisees—a Jewish sect or party which insisted on a rigorous observance of the Law. These men were very hostile toward Jesus.

Pontius Pilate—Roman governor of Palestine who, at the request of the Jewish leaders, ordered Jesus' death.

Sadducees—a political party within the Judaism of Jesus' time, concentrated among the priests and Temple leaders.

Salome—daughter of Herodias, who asked for the head of John the Baptist on a platter.

Salome, mother of James and John—present at the crucifixion of Jesus.

Scribes—the learned Jewish people of Jesus' day who were called Rabbi.

Simeon—a Temple prophet who recognized Jesus' special role, even while Jesus was only an infant.

Simon of Cyrene—man forced to carry Jesus' cross to Calvary.

Zacchaeus—a tax collector who climbed into a tree to see Jesus and later changed his life to follow him.

Zechariah—father of John the Baptist.

Finding Gospel Passages

In medieval times, scholars had a very hard time communicating with one another about passages in the Bible. To make things easier, they divided each book of the New and Old Testaments into chapters and gave each chapter a number. Then, they took each sentence or so in each chapter and gave it a number, too. By giving three bits of information, they could zero in on one single sentence in the whole Bible.

Let's take an example: **John 2:1–12**

1. The word "John" tells me to turn to the Gospel according to John.

2. The number before the colon (in this case, 2) tells me which chapter of John to look in. Now I am in the second chapter of John's gospel.

3. The numbers after the colon tell me which verses to begin and end with in that second chapter. In this case I begin with the first verse and read down through the twelfth verse. Now, try looking up John 2:1–12 and see what story you find.

The *references* printed in small type either in the margins of the text or at the bottom of the page are called *cross references.* They indicate other places in the Bible where the same or similar passages can be found.

Check the first of the Beatitudes (Matthew 5:3).

In some editions of the Bible, the cross references mention here the 19th chapter of Matthew, where several stories illustrate the point of the Beatitude, and to 2 Corinthians 8:9, which tells us that Jesus became poor for our sake.

Footnotes are also a feature of most modern Bibles. They explain why passages are translated as they are and what scholars think they mean.

Gospel Parables

A parable is a story whose meaning is not immediately obvious. Parables take a little pondering to get into the meat of their meaning. Jesus, like many Oriental sages, loved the parable. It allowed him to talk about a profound truth in words that did not frighten simple people. At their own speed and in their own way, they would probe the story and, when ready, uncover its meaning. A parable might sit on the edge of one's mind for years before being understood. On the other hand, someone else might understand it almost immediately.

Here are some of Jesus' most remembered parables, where you can find them in the gospels, and a hint of what they may mean to you.

The Salt of the Earth MATTHEW 5:13
Jesus' followers add an invisible yet essential ingredient to human history.

The Light of the World MATTHEW 5:14–16
We who follow Jesus are overcoming the world's evil.

The Sower MATTHEW 13:4–9
Not everyone who hears Jesus' message does something about it.

The Wheat and the Weeds MATTHEW 13:24–30
Good and evil will exist side by side, often appearing much alike.

The Mustard Seed MATTHEW 13:31–32
Goodness will overcome evil.

The Net MATTHEW 13:47–50
God's justice will win out.

The Lost Sheep MATTHEW 18:12–14
God cares about sinners. No one is outside God's love.

The Unforgiving Debtor MATTHEW 18:23–35
God cannot forgive us if we do not forgive one another.

The Vineyard Laborers—MATTHEW 20:1–16
God's ways are very different from ours.

The Two Sons MATTHEW 21:28–32
No sinner is so evil God does not love him or her.

The Wicked Farmers MATTHEW 21:33–46
Those who reject God's love will be punished.

The Wedding Feast MATTHEW 22:1–14
We will meet the most unlikely people in heaven.

The Ten Bridesmaids MATTHEW 25:1–13
We must be alert to the opportunities God gives us.

The Talents MATTHEW 25:14–30
To whom much has been given much will be expected.

The Sheep and the Goats MATTHEW 25:31–46
We serve God best by caring for our neighbors.

The Good Samaritan LUKE 10:29–37
Life's outcasts are often God's closest friends.

The Insistent Friend LUKE 11:5–8
God does hear our prayers.

The Prodigal Son LUKE 15:11–32
God is always waiting for us to repent.

The Pharisee and the Publican LUKE 18:9–14
Humility is a cornerstone of holiness.

The Name of Jesus

From the time of Saint Paul, Christians have revered the name of Jesus. Some people today still bow their heads at the mention of his name.

The name Jesus means "God saves." It is a variant of Joshua and a common name in some places. Because people had no last names as we do, it was necessary to distinguish among the many people who shared the same name. In

Nazareth, Jesus was known as Jesus bar-Joseph, Jesus son of Joseph. Outside of Nazareth, he was called Jesus the Nazarene or Jesus of Nazareth.

After his resurrection, Jesus' followers called him the Christ, the Messiah, the one anointed by God to save all humankind. The title was a favorite one among ancient Jews who longed for the coming of the Christ or Messiah. To get the flavor of this expression in English we might better say "Jesus, the Christ."

The Way of the Cross

We learn as much about Jesus through prayer as we do by study. Through the centuries Christians have found many imaginative ways to enter into the mysteries of Jesus' life. One of the most popular is the Way of the Cross.

Christians have always wanted to reflect on the sufferings which marked the final moments of Jesus' life. For centuries they made pilgrimages to Jerusalem and there retraced his final steps to Calvary. When Jerusalem fell into the hands of unfriendly Muslims and pilgrimages there were impossible, the church began to encourage people to continue the tradition of meditating on fourteen events which tradition remembers happening during the last hours of Jesus' life.

These are the traditional Stations of the Cross.

1. Jesus is condemned by Pilate.

2. Jesus accepts his cross.

3. Jesus falls the first time.

4. Jesus meets his mother.

5. Simon of Cyrene helps Jesus carry his cross.

6. Veronica wipes the face of Jesus.

7. Jesus falls the second time.

8. Jesus speaks to the weeping women.

9. Jesus falls the third time.

10. Jesus is stripped of his garments.

11. Jesus is crucified.

12. Jesus dies on the cross.

13. Jesus is taken from the cross.

14. Jesus is buried in the sepulcher.

In recent years popes have asked us to add a reflection on Jesus' resurrection since our reflections on his suffering and death are incomplete without pondering the mystery of his resurrection.

Here are Pope John Paul II's Scripture Stations of the Cross:

1. Jesus prays in the Garden of Olives. (Luke 22:39–46)

2. Jesus is betrayed by Judas. (Matthew 26:45–49)

3. Jesus is condemned to death by the Sanhedrin. (Mark 14:56,61–64)

4. Jesus is denied by Peter. (Luke 22:54–62)

5. Jesus is judged by Pilate. (Luke 23:20–25)

6. Jesus is flogged and crowned with thorns. (John 19:1–3)

7. Jesus carries his cross. (John 19:17)

8. Jesus is helped by Simon of Cyrene. (Mark 15:20–21)

9. Jesus encounters the women of Jerusalem. (Luke 23:39–43)

10. Jesus is crucified. (Mark 15:22–26)

11. Jesus promises to share his reign with the good thief. (Luke 23:39–43)

12. Jesus is on the cross, with his mother and disciple below. (John 19:25–27)

13. Jesus dies on the cross. (Matthew 27:45–50)

14. Jesus is placed in the tomb. (Matthew 27:57–61)

15. Jesus is raised from the dead. (John 20:1–10)

Jesus' Heritage

Jesus was a man of his time and of his people. When he was no more than a boy he learned the history of his people, their wisdom literature, and, perhaps most important, the sometimes anguished cries of the prophets. To understand and appreciate Jesus, we must return to these ancient Jewish books for it is on them Jesus based much of his teaching.

Catholic Christians, like members of other Christian churches, love the Bible as Jesus did. This book is a wonderful possession, one with roots in the ancient past that is a collection of writings by some of the world's most interesting religious personalities.

This section of *Basics of the Catholic Faith* opens up some of this treasure to you.

The Bible

Any search for Jesus takes us to the Bible, to the writings that helped form his childhood faith. Today we call these writings the Jewish Scriptures or the Old Testament.

The word Bible comes from the Greek word *biblios,* for book. It is the official collection of writings which believers accept as the authentic word of God. Over the centuries first the Jewish community and later the Christian church decided which ancient writings were to be included in the Bible. The Bible is not only the word of God but the work of the communities of faith as well.

Christians and Jews are sometimes called "people of the Book." We reverence this holy collection and believe that God inspired its authors. Jews and Christians alike base their religious beliefs on their sacred Scriptures.

Few of us are able to read the ancient languages in which these books were originally written or know much about the subtleties of their cultural and historical context which so influence their meaning. Our best guide in understanding the Bible is the living church with all its resources and its centuries of experience.

The Old Testament

Following Jesus inevitably creates in us a desire to understand the religious culture in which he lived. Because the Jewish people preserved their heritage, we know a great deal about what happened to the Jewish people in the time before Jesus. We find this information in that collection of the forty-six ancient writings of the Old Testament.

The Pentateuch
The first five books of the Bible are called the Pentateuch (which means five), and they explore human origins, God's choice of the Hebrew people, the covenant or treaty God made

with them, and the Law which was Israel's obligation under the covenant. Originally oral traditions, these books were written and rewritten over hundreds of years. They define Hebrew identity and are the foundation of all Hebrew life.

1. The Book of Genesis *(stories that lead to God's choice of Israel as his special people)*

2. The Book of Exodus *(stories of God's deliverance of Israel and his covenant with them)*

3. The Book of Leviticus *(rules and regulations for living in the covenant)*

4. The Book of Numbers *(more rules, regulations, and the stories behind them)*

5. The Book of Deuteronomy *(stories of Israel's entry into the Promised Land)*

The Historical Books
These sixteen books recount many of the high points of Hebrew history from the entry into Palestine to within a century of Jesus' coming. Ancient peoples did not write history as we do. They told stories, recorded sermons, and tried to explain why things happened as they did. These historical books include:

1. Joshua
2. Judges
3. Ruth
4. First Samuel
5. Second Samuel
6. First Kings
7. Second Kings
8. First Chronicles
9. Second Chronicles
10. Ezra
11. Nehemiah
12. Tobit
13. Judith
14. Esther
15. First Maccabees
16. Second Maccabees

The Wisdom Books
These are seven books of poems, prayers, practical advice, and wise sayings.

1. Job
2. Psalms
3. Proverbs
4. Ecclesiastes
5. Song of Songs
6. Wisdom
7. Sirach

The Prophets

These eighteen books contain the poems, pronouncements, and stories of the prophets, people called by God to deliver his message to Israel. Prophets had no official standing in Israel. They had only their lives and their message to recommend them. Jesus and John the Baptist were considered prophets by many of their contemporaries. The prophetic books include:

1. Isaiah	7. Hosea	13. Nahum
2. Jeremiah	8. Joel	14. Habakkuk
3. Lamentations	9. Amos	15. Zephaniah
4. Baruch	10. Obadiah	16. Haggai
5. Ezekiel	11. Jonah	17. Zechariah
6. Daniel	12. Micah	18. Malachi

▮ The New Testament

Anyone searching for Jesus will turn to the Christian Scriptures or the "New Testament," a collection of twenty-seven documents written by early disciples of Jesus probably during the second half of the first century. The word "testament" means a treaty or covenant agreement between God and all who believe in Jesus, just as the "Old Testament" is a treaty between God and the Israelites. Scholars don't always know exactly when each book was written or who the authors were, even though tradition assigns a specific disciple as the author of each book.

The Gospels

These are four collections of the sayings and actions of Jesus, woven together around the main events of his life. They include:

1. The Gospel according to Matthew *(written between 70 and 75 A.D.)*

2. The Gospel according to Mark *(written between 65 and 70 A.D.)*

3. The Gospel according to Luke *(written between 70 and 80 A.D.)*

4. The Gospel according to John *(written between 90 and 99 A.D.)*

The Acts of the Apostles
This is an intriguing view of the first disciples and the early journeys of Saint Paul written by Saint Luke, probably about the same time as his version of the gospel (70 to 80 A.D.).

The Letters of Saint Paul
These are letters that Saint Paul wrote to different communities of faith and to other Christian missionaries.

1. Romans—*written about 58 A.D. to the church in Rome*

2. 1 Corinthians—*written about 57 A.D. to the church in Corinth*

3. 2 Corinthians—*written about 57 A.D. to the church in Corinth*

4. Galatians—*written about 58 A.D. to the church in Galacia*

5. Ephesians—*written about 62 A.D. to the church in Ephesus*

6. Philippians—*written about 56 A.D. to the church in Philippi*

7. Colossians—*written about 62 A.D. to the church in Colossia*

8. 1 Thessalonians—*written about 50 A.D. to the church in Thessalonika*

9. 2 Thessalonians—*written about 51 A.D. to the church in Thessalonika*

10. 1 Timothy—*written about 65 A.D. to his coworker Timothy*

11. 2 Timothy—*written about 65 A.D. to his coworker Timothy*

12. Titus—*written about 65 A.D. to his coworker Titus*

13. Philemon—*written about 62 A.D. to a fellow believer, Philemon*

14. Hebrews—*written about 67 A.D. to Hebrew Christians*

Letters to all Christians
These are letters by early church leaders that probably were written to be circulated to several churches.

1. James—The letter of James *(written shortly before 62 A.D.)*

2. 1 Peter—First letter of Peter *(written shortly before 62 A.D.)*

3. 2 Peter—Second letter of Peter *(written at the end of the first century)*

4. 1 John—First letter of John *(written about 90 A.D.)*

5. 2 John—Second letter of John *(written about 90 A.D.)*

6. 3 John—Third letter of John *(written about 90 A.D.)*

7. Jude—The letter of Jude *(written between 65 and 70 A.D.)*

The Book of Revelation
This final book of the Bible was written in sometimes obscure symbolic language to encourage those early Christians who were undergoing persecution. It was probably written toward the end of the first century.

▌Favorite New Testament Passages

They devoted themselves to the apostles' teaching and fellowship, to the breaking of bread and the prayers.   ACTS 2:42

They would sell their possessions and goods and distribute the proceeds to all, as any had need. Day by day, as they spent much time together in the temple, they broke bread at home and ate their food with glad and generous hearts.

ACTS 2:45–46

And every day in the temple and at home they did not cease to teach and proclaim Jesus as the Messiah.   ACTS 5:42

"Saul, Saul, why do you persecute me?" He asked, "Who are you, Lord?" The reply came, "I am Jesus, whom you are persecuting."

ACTS 9:4–5

"Lord Jesus, receive my spirit." Then he knelt down and cried out in a loud voice, "Lord, do not hold this sin against them." When he had said this, he died. And Saul approved of their killing him. ACTS 7:59—8:1

Now there are varieties of gifts, but the same Spirit; and there are varieties of services, but the same Lord; and there are varieties of activities, but it is the same God who activates all of them in everyone. 1 CORINTHIANS 12:4–6

Listen, my beloved brothers and sisters. Has not God chosen the poor in the world to be rich in faith and to be heirs of the kingdom that he has promised to those who love him? JAMES 2:5

Now you are the body of Christ and individually members of it. 1 CORINTHIANS 12:27

We know that all things work together for good for those who love God, who are called according to his purpose. ROMANS 8:28

Now by this we may be sure that we know him, if we obey his commandments. 1 JOHN 2:3

Let love be genuine; hate what is evil, hold fast to what is good; love one another with mutual affection; outdo one another in showing honor. ROMANS 12:9–10

Church Approval

As we search for Jesus in the Bible we want to be sure that the English translation we have and the footnotes that help us understand the text are accurate. The church provides us with this service.

Church leaders routinely check new Bible translations and certify that they contain no doctrinal error. Since few of us have the education or the leisure to check every word of every translation, this service of the hierarchy is an important one.

The guarantee (like the Good Housekeeping Seal of Approval) is stylized. It appears either at the beginning or end of the Bible and begins with the Latin word "Imprimatur" followed by the name of a bishop who made the investigation. The word "Imprimatur" means "it may be printed."

Bible Studies

Study of the Bible is a science and so has specialized words of its own. Here are some of the more common ones you may encounter:

Inspiration—the process by which God protected and guided Bible writers.

Pentateuch—the first five Bible books, which express the Hebrew ideal of law and covenant.

Law—a collection of rules of conduct for individuals, groups, families, and the proper conduct of worship that form the backbone of the Hebrew tradition. This collection includes the Ten Commandments. Jesus insisted that he had not come to change it but to bring it to fulfillment.

Covenant—God's solemn promise to the people of Israel and later to the followers of Jesus.

Canon—the official list of accepted writings. Protestants and Catholics each have a slightly different canon.

A Book of the Bible—a writing that is self-contained or that used to occupy one entire scroll. Books as we know them are much more modern than the Bible. All ancient writings used to be rolled up in scrolls.

Textual criticism—scholarly work that attempts to determine the most authentic ancient texts.

Biblical forms—the taken-for-granted literary rules Bible writers followed when composing their books.

Fundamentalist—a person who believes each passage in the Bible should be taken literally. The Catholic church rejects this position.

Messiah—Hebrew word which means the "anointed one" and usually meant the one whom God would anoint and send into the world to initiate an era of peace and prosperity. The word "Christ" is the English equivalent.

Exegesis—A systematic study of ancient biblical manuscripts to determine what their author meant when he wrote them. Scholars use linguistics, history, and comparison with other texts to get at the true meaning of the passage.

Bible History

The history of Jesus' people is a long one stretching back over many centuries. Those who wrote about that history did so in ways very different from the way modern historians write. They were less interested in the what, where, and when of an event than in why that event happened and its significance for believers.

The stories about human beginnings (Adam and Eve, Cain and Abel, Noah, and the Tower of Babel) in the first chapters of the Book of Genesis are not set in historical time. They are parable-type stories that contain deep theological truths but are not necessarily related to actual happenings. Historical time begins with Abraham whose story begins in the twelfth chapter of the Book of Genesis.

Notice how the year numbers before Jesus decrease as the centuries roll on and increase after his birth. Thus, 1,000 B.C. is earlier than 900 B.C. but 50 A.D. is earlier than 60 A.D.

All dates below, unless noted otherwise, are B.C. and approximate.

1850—Abraham arrived in Palestine.

1700—Joseph and his brothers entered Egypt.

1250—Moses led Hebrews out of Egypt.

1200—The Judges ruled Palestine.

1040—The loose tribal organization of Israel gave way to a monarchy. This was the time of Samuel, Saul, Jonathan, David, and Solomon.

931—After Solomon's death. the kingdom was divided into two rival monarchies: Israel, which included the ten northern tribes, and Judah, which included the two southern tribes. This was the age of such prophets as Elijah, Elisha, Amos, and Hosea.

721—After two centuries of poor leadership and lessening religious interest, the Northern Kingdom (Israel) was taken into captivity and never returned. We call the people who lived there "the ten lost tribes."

587—Jerusalem, the capital of Judah, fell, as the prophet Jeremiah had predicted. The Temple and the entire city were destroyed and the people were taken into captivity to Babylon.

538—Babylon in turn fell to the Persian armies. Their king, Cyrus, allowed the Jews to return and rebuild Jerusalem.

250-150—After years of comparative peace under Persian and Greek rule, active persecution began again in Jerusalem. The Maccabee family led a heroic Jewish resistance.

Between 7 and 1 B.C.—Jesus was born in Bethlehem. (Because of an error in computation, Jesus may have been born several years earlier than originally believed.)

The following dates are A.D. and they too are approximate.

7 A.D.	Birth of Paul
30 A.D.	Death of Jesus Coming of the Holy Spirit at Pentecost
36 A.D.	Death of Saint Stephen, the first martyr Conversion of Saint Paul
43 A.D.	Paul and Barnabas at Antioch
44 A.D.	Beheading of Saint James in Jerusalem
45-49 A.D.	First missionary journey of Saint Paul

50–52 A.D.	Second missionary journey of Saint Paul
53–58 A.D.	Third missionary journey of Saint Paul
58 A.D.	Saint Paul in Jerusalem
58–60 A.D.	Saint Paul captive in Palestine
61–63 A.D.	Saint Paul captive in Rome
63 A.D.	Saint Paul set free and may have visited Spain
67 A.D.	Saints Peter and Paul are martyred in Rome
70 A.D.	Destruction of Jerusalem by the Romans Dispersion of Jews and Jewish Christians
100 A.D.	Saint John, the last of the apostles, died and thus ended the biblical era.

Bible Resources

Five kinds of books can help you study the Bible and gain a deeper appreciation of the life and times of Jesus.

A **Bible Commentary** is a book that gives background information and interpretation for each verse in the whole Bible or one or more Bible books.

Bible Dictionaries list all important topics in the Bible. Each idea is explained in some detail by Bible scholars.

A **Textual Concordance** lists every word in the Bible arranged in alphabetical order. You can use it to help you find half-remembered quotations.

A **Thematic Concordance** lists many quotations from the Bible arranged under important titles.

A **Harmony** of the Gospels prints passages from all four gospels in parallel columns so readers can see at a glance the relationship among them.

Bible Heroes and Heroines

All of the following people were part of Jesus' religious heritage.

Abraham—The first in a long line of historical figures with whom God made a covenant.

Isaac—The son of Abraham and Sarah, a man who kept alive the promise made to his father by God.

Jacob—A twin son of Isaac and Rebecca. He tricked his twin brother, Esau, and inherited the promise. He labored for years to obtain the hand of Rachel in marriage and he fathered the twelve patriarchs who gave their names to the tribes of Israel or Jacob.

Joseph—One of Jacob's sons who was sold into slavery by his brothers, but who eventually saved his family from famine by bringing them to Egypt.

Moses—With his brother, Aaron, he challenged Egyptian power and led the Hebrews out of Egypt into the desert. He gave the Hebrews the laws he received from God and organized the nation.

Joshua—He led the Israelites out of the desert and into Palestine where they conquered the native Canaanites.

The Judges—These were early rulers of the Israelites in Palestine. They arose when needed and then faded into the background. At that time the tribes had no clear central organization and they relied on the Judges to lead them.

Samson—The most popular of all the Judges who fought against the newly arrived Philistines.

Ruth—A woman who provides a link between the days of

the Judges and the monarchy of the Israelites.

Samuel—The last of the Judges who witnessed the transition to the monarchy, which he opposed.

Saul—Anointed by Samuel the first king of Israel, he was later rejected and died in battle.

David—The heroic second king of Israel. As a boy he killed the Philistine giant Goliath. Later he was outlawed by Saul. Upon Saul's death, he became king of Israel and extended its boundaries in all directions. Many of the biblical psalms are attributed to David.

Solomon—He was David's son who became Israel's king and a man known to have an "understanding heart." Later in life, he turned away from the Lord. Upon his death, his kingdom was divided into two competing monarchies, one headquartered in Jerusalem and the other in Samaria.

Elijah—The first of a long line of men and women we call prophets who delivered messages from the Lord and called on Israel to put its faith into practice. Elijah opposed the kings of Samaria, then a part of Israel, and their injustice and worship of false gods.

Elisha—The successor of Elijah, he was a man of miracles and outspoken opposition to false worship and injustice.

Amos—He was a humble farmer called by God to speak against the luxury and injustice of the people in the Samarian court.

Hosea—A prophet who had a faithless wife, Hosea wrote of Israel as the faithless bride of God.

Jeremiah—He was a man called by God to guide Jerusalem through the final days before its destruction by the

Babylonians. He was hated by Jerusalem's ruling class and probably died in Egyptian exile.

Isaiah—A prophet who lived just before and during the Babylonian exile, Isaiah's poetry is filled with hope.

Daniel—This is a mythical character whose name is given to one of the biblical books that encouraged Jews during one of their most terrifying persecutions.

Job—Because he struggled with the problem of why bad things happen to good people, Job is an example of faith and trust.

Esther—She was a great popular heroine of the Jews during their persecutions.

Judith—Another popular heroine, Judith led the Jews to victory over their enemies.

The Maccabees—They were a Jewish family who led a resistance movement against the pagan rulers who attempted to obliterate their religion and culture in the second century B.C.

Favorite Old Testament Passages

I call heaven and earth to witness against you today that I have set before you life and death, blessings and curses. Choose life so that you and your descendants may live...

DEUTERONOMY 30:19

The Lord is my rock, my fortress, and my deliverer, my God, my rock, in who I take refuge.   2 SAMUEL 22:2-3

I will bless those who bless you, and the one who curses you I will curse; and in you all the families of the earth shall be blessed.   GENESIS 12:3

So Jacob served seven years for Rachel, and they seemed to him but a few days because of the love he had for her.

GENESIS 29:20

Obey my voice, and I will be your God, and you shall be my people; and walk only in the way that I command you, so that it may be well with you.   JEREMIAH 7:23

But Ruth said, "Do not press me to leave you or to turn back from following you! Where you go, I will go; where you lodge, I will lodge; your people shall be my people, and your God my God. Where you die, I will die—there will I be buried. May the LORD do thus and so to me, and more as well, if even death parts me from you!" When Naomi saw that she was determined to go with her, she said no more to her.   RUTH 1:16-18

The LORD is my shepherd, I shall not want. He makes me lie down in green pastures; he leads me beside still waters.

PSALM 23:1–2

Comfort, O comfort my people, says your God. Speak tenderly to Jerusalem, and cry to her that she has served her term, that her penalty is paid.

ISAIAH 40:1–2

Have mercy on me, O God, according to your steadfast love; according to your abundant mercy blot out my transgressions. Wash me thoroughly from my iniquity, and cleanse me from my sin.

PSALM 51:1–2

Focus on
the Church

Twenty centuries of living with the gospel of Jesus is a long time, time to accumulate traditions, heroes, customs, special words, and an intricate system of relationships. This section of *Basics of the Catholic Faith* is about this two thousand-year-old heritage and the people who have been part of it. Also included are quotations from the early church itself.

To be comfortable in any community—from a nation to a neighborhood—we need to know four things: the community's language, its special words and expressions, how it came to be, and its customs and way of behaving.

The Catholic church is no exception. A relationship with Jesus is only the beginning. We believers are, in the words of Jesus, like a living vine with its many branches all pulsing with the same Spirit's life and so inexorably tied to one another.

Church Organization

We follow Jesus not alone but in community. Our community, the Roman Catholic church, is both ancient and modern. Understanding all its organizational subtleties can be a challenge.

The Catholic church is an organized community of faith. With twenty centuries of history behind it and scores of reforms and renewals in its past, the church has evolved a very complicated and perhaps confusing structure. In spite of its complexity, church organization works well and provides most church members with a maximum of freedom and strong support in time of need.

The International Church

The Pope—chief administrator and teacher of the world church, bishop of the diocese of Rome, patriarch of the Latin Rite, head of the college of bishops, and ruler of the tiny independent country, the Vatican State.

Curia—officials who help the pope in his work of teaching, governing, and administering. The Secretariat of State, for example, maintains diplomatic relations with many countries and often negotiates with heads of state concerning the religious rights of their own citizens. There are also congregations for such works as: worship, canonization of saints, the clergy, religious, education, and evangelization. Other offices are called secretariats, tribunals, commissions, and institutes. They deal with a variety of concerns from promoting Christian unity to disputes between dioceses, from matters of justice and peace to financial administration. All are responsible to the pope.

College of Cardinals—a group of men, appointed to a life term by the pope, who meet to elect the next pope and occasionally to give the pope advice on important matters. Individual cardinals hold many diverse offices in the church. Some work in the Roman curia while others are heads of important dioceses throughout the world. Centuries ago, the cardinals were the bishops near Rome, the pastors of certain Roman churches, and deacons in Rome. This tradition is still maintained by calling some cardinal bishops, others cardinal priests, and others cardinal deacons.

The Synod of Bishops—bishops around the world elect representatives and send them to Rome every third year to dialogue with the pope on important matters such as Christian marriage, the need for vocations, the role of women.

Ecumenical Council—a meeting of all the bishops of the world held to clarify matters of belief or to give direction to church policy. There have been only twenty such councils in the history of the church. The most recent was the Second Vatican Council (Vatican II) held in the 1960s.

Religious Communities—men and/or women who have joined together to live lives dedicated to Jesus and the church through public vows of poverty, chastity, and obedience. These religious orders or communities often serve in many different countries and maintain a worldwide office in Rome.

The Regional Church

National Conferences of Bishops—the bishops in individual countries (or groups of countries when they are very small) meet regularly to coordinate policy on matters that affect all their members. They elect a president, usually have a permanent staff to carry out their policies, and elect representatives to the world synod held every third year in Rome. The pope keeps in contact with the bishops of a country through a representative usually called the "apostolic delegate."

The Province—a group of dioceses that share common concerns because they are close to one another. The bishop of the largest or oldest diocese in the province is called an archbishop and his diocese an archdiocese. Bishops, priests, and laypeople often meet on the provincial level to discuss common problems and opportunities.

The Diocesan Church

The Bishop—the shepherd of all who live in his diocese is called the "ordinary" of that diocese. He may be assisted by other "auxiliary bishops." If it has been agreed that one of these auxiliary bishops will succeed the ordinary when he dies or retires, this person is called a "coadjutor." The bishop is also associated with one church in his diocese, which is called the cathedral.

The Chancery—a group of priests, deacons, sisters, brothers, and laypeople who help the bishop in his work. The bishop's first assistant is called a "vicar general." Others may help with finances and management (the chancellor), education, charity, priests' assignments, marriage preparation, liturgy, evangelization, etc. Their task is to provide research and specialized services for the parishes of the diocese.

Commissions and Committees—most bishops are advised by a large number of commissions and committees, from a school board to a priests' senate, from a sisters' senate to a pastoral council, from a charities commission to a liturgy commission. The number and kind of these groups vary from diocese to diocese.

The Diocesan Tribunal—a group of canon lawyers who specialize in church law, especially marriage annulments. Each diocese has an "officialis" or chief judge, other judges, advocates, defenders of the marriage bond. The tribunal holds regular sessions at which testimony is considered and verdicts handed down. All diocesan verdicts are automatically appealed to a second court before they become official.

Diocesan and Regional Institutions—many schools, hospitals, and other specialized institutions owned by the diocese are operated on an interparochial basis. They serve and are financially assisted by more than one parish.

Religious Orders—most dioceses have schools and other institutions that are owned by religious orders, not by the diocese. They are responsible to the bishop for teaching true doctrine and for their conduct of public prayer but otherwise operate independently.

The Parish Church

The Pastor—the chief administrator and teacher of the local church. He may be helped by other priests called "parochial vicars" and/or by a variety of others: deacons, pastoral assistants, ministers to the sick, directors of religious education, ministers of music, social service coordinators, etc.

The Parish Council—most parishes today have an advisory group selected from the parish to assist the pastor and other parish employees.

Parish Societies—most societies are directly responsible to the pastor. One notable exception is the Knights of Columbus. They work closely with their pastors but are not a part of the church's official organization.

Special People and Places

Honorary Titles—The Vatican confers honors on individuals who have given valuable service to the church. A bishop may be called "an archbishop" even though his diocese is not an archdiocese. A priest may be given the title "monsignor." Laypeople may be made Knights of Saint Gregory or of Malta.

Seminaries—specialized schools for training men for the priesthood. They exist on the high school, college, and graduate school levels. The graduate level schools are often called "theologates."

Church Buildings with special beauty or importance in the history of the church are called basilicas.

Heads of Religious Communities—use many different titles from abbot and abbess to general (head of the whole order) and provincial (head of a part or province of the order).

More About the Parish

A parish is a community of believers headed by a priest called the pastor. It is here that most people find the support and help they need in their following of Jesus.

Parishes provide many helps to those seeking a deeper and richer spiritual life.

Worship—Every Sunday and most weekdays members of the community celebrate the Lord's Supper together. These gatherings are commonly called "the liturgy" or "the Mass." Everyone is welcome.

Special sacraments—Sacraments mark watershed times in the lives of believers and are celebrated in the parish, often during the Sunday liturgy.

Care of the sick—Holy Communion, Bible readings, and prayers provide worship opportunities in hospitals, nursing homes, and residences of those too ill or infirm to celebrate with the whole community of parishioners are an important part of parish life. They include novenas in honor of Jesus, Mary, or favorite saints, prayer groups, the rosary, the way of the cross, retreats, missions, and other prayer opportunities Catholics treasure.

Counseling—Most parishes provide special programs for people about to be married, for couples who are searching for ways to enrich their marriages, for individuals who are trying to reform their lives and to many who are troubled. The Sacrament of Penance (also called Confession and Reconciliation) provides an opportunity for people to talk over their goals and progress toward them with a priest.

Devotions—Prayer services with appeal to special groups of parishioners are an important part of parish life. They include novenas in honor of Jesus, Mary, or favorite saints, prayer groups, the rosary, the way of the cross, retreats, missions, and other prayer opportunities Catholics treasure.

Education—There are a wide variety of educational opportunities open to parishioners of most parishes. Some provide Catholic schools for youth. Most have special religious education programs for children, youth ministry opportunities for teens, and special adult offerings for older parishioners as well as parish-wide efforts during Lent, Advent, and at other special times during the year.

Service—Most parishes have service groups like the Saint Vincent de Paul Society or the Legion of Mary and encourage all parishioners to participate in supporting a variety of worthy causes. More and more parishes combine local service with a study of the underlying causes of social problems like poverty, violence, hopelessness, racial conflicts, disintegration of families, etc. As a result, many Catholics become politically active in reform movements.

Community-building—Church suppers, parties, parent-teen programs and a variety of other activities help promote a deepening of parish community. In addition, many parish societies have a strong social dimension with regular meetings and many fund-raising activities.

Leadership—Parishioners may work with their parish staff by serving as officers of various parish societies, on the parish council and other governing boards, as lectors and communion ministers at Mass, as ministers to the sick, as liturgy planners, in the parish music program, and in many other leadership roles.

Growth—One of the parish's most important tasks is to deepen its own awareness of the impact of the gospel of Jesus on current topics like war and peace, nuclear arms, human rights, world hunger, abortion, pornography, and the use of money. Homilies, special programs, discussions, and distribution of literature all help in this kind of growth. While different parishioners may hold different opinions on these topics, all are expected to respect the opinions of others and to try to learn from interacting with them.

Catholic Heroes and Heroines

Christians have always treasured the memory of men and women whose lives were an inspiration to the whole community.

Here is a list of some of the more popular saints and the ages in which they lived.

The First Century: age of our Christian beginnings
Saint Peter—*the leader of the apostles, martyred in Rome*
Saint Paul—*apostle to the Gentiles, also martyred in Rome*
Saint Mary Magdalene—*friend of Jesus*
Saint Clement—*pope and defender of church unity*

The Second Century: an era of growth
Saint Ignatius—*bishop of Antioch, writer, martyr*
Saint Polycarp—*bishop, martyr, disciple of Saint John*

The Third Century: an era of intense persecution
Saint Cecilia—*martyr and patroness of church music*
Saint Lawrence—*deacon, friend of the poor*

The Fourth Century: Christianity becomes official
Saint Anthony—*founder of Egyptian monastic life*
Saint Martin of Tours—*apostle to France*
Saint Augustine—*North African theologian and bishop*
Saint Nicholas—*whom we honor today as Santa Claus*
Saint Agnes—*teenage martyr of Rome*
Saint Jerome—*biblical scholar and hermit*
Saint Ambrose—*theologian and bishop*
Saint Monica—*mystic and mother of Saint Augustine*

The Fifth Century: invasion of Europe by barbarian tribes
Saint John Chrysostom—*defender of the Trinity*
Saint Patrick—*apostle to Ireland*
Saint Brigid of Ireland—*founder of monasteries for men and for women*
Saint Genevieve—*protector of Paris from Hun invaders*
Saint Hilary—*popular saint who was once excommunicated*

The Sixth Century: an era of new beginnings

Saint Benedict—*founder of monastic life in Europe*
Saint Scholastica—*sister of Benedict and herself a religious leader*

The Seventh Century: a time of conflict

Saint Cuthbert—*English missionary bishop*
Saint Oswald—*king of Scotland*

The Eighth Century: an era of reform and confusion

Saint John Damascene—*teacher, writer, and mystic*
Saint Boniface—*apostle to the German peoples*

The Ninth Century: Europe's attempt to reorganize

Saint Ansgar—*apostle to Scandinavia*
Saints Cyril and Methodius—*apostles to the Slavic peoples*

The Tenth Century: Europe's darkest age

Saint Olga—*grandduchess of Kiev and mother of Russian Christianity*
Saint Stephen—*apostle to Hungary*

The Eleventh Century: end of the dark ages

Saint Anselm—*teacher, theologian, and counselor*
Saint Ladislaus—*king of Poland and early advocate of religious liberty*
Saint Peter Damian—*monk and church reformer who became
    a cardinal only when threatened with excommunication if
    he refused to honor the appointment*

The Twelfth Century: beginning of a new era

Saint Bernard of Clairvaux—*reformer, writer, advocate
    of devotion to Mary*
Saint Thomas Becket—*English archbishop martyred in his
    own cathedral*
Saint Hildegard—*called wisest woman of her age*

The Thirteenth Century: an age of scholars and saints

Saint Francis of Assisi—*poet, mystic, friend of the poor*
Saint Dominic—*mystic, preacher, and reformer*
Saint Clare—*founder of the Poor Clares*
Saint Anthony of Padua—*teacher and preacher*
Saint Gertrude—*mystic and first to propose devotion
    to the Sacred Heart*

Saint Albert the Great—*teacher and scientific pioneer*
Saint Thomas Aquinas—*considered by many the greatest
 theologian in Christian history*
Saint Bonaventure—*mystic and theologian*

The Fourteenth Century: beginning of a decline

Saint Brigid—*Swedish queen and reformer*
Saint Catherine of Siena—*counselor to popes, mystic*

The Fifteenth Century: an era of decline

Saint Catherine of Genoa—*widow and renowned teacher*
Saint Joan of Arc—*French military leader burned at the stake*

The Sixteenth Century: Christianity divided in Europe

Saint Thomas More—*chancellor of England and martyr*
Saint John Fisher—*bishop martyred in the Reformation conflict*
Saint Teresa of Avila—*Spanish mystic and reformer*
Saint Ignatius of Loyola—*founder of the Jesuits*
Saint John of the Cross—*mystic and reformer*
Saint Philip Neri—*apostle to poor children in Rome*

The Seventeenth Century: time of secularization in Europe

Saint Vincent de Paul—*organizer of charities*
Saint Francis de Sales—*writer and spiritual guide*
Saint Peter Claver—*apostle to slaves being brought to the Americas*
Saint Margaret Mary Alacoque—*apostle of devotion
 to the Sacred Heart*
Saint Isaac Jogues—*martyr and apostle to native Americans*
Saint Martin de Porres—*heroic worker among slaves
 and outcasts in Peru*

The Eighteenth Century:
the era of petty persecution in Europe

Saint Benedict Joseph Labre—*pilgrim and mystic*
Saint Paul of the Cross—*mystic and leader of church reform*
Saint Alphonsus Ligouri—*apostle to the forgotten Italian poor*

The Nineteenth Century: beginnings of a Catholic revival

Saint John Bosco—*apostle to the poor*
Saint Elizabeth Seton—*American widow and founder
 of Catholic schools*

Saint John Vianney—*French pastor and mystic*
Saint Bernadette—*visionary and mystic*
Saint Thérèse of Lisieux—*mystic and popular writer*
Saint John Neumann—*American bishop and promoter of Catholic schools*
Damian of Molokai—*apostle to the lepers*

The Twentieth Century—a time of flowering

Saint Pius X —*pope and reformer*
Matt Talbot—*former alcoholic and Irish mystic*
Charles de Foucauld—*former soldier of fortune and hermit*
John XXIII—*pope, father of Vatican II and most loved Catholic leader of our era*
Katharine Drexel—*apostle to American Blacks and Indians*
Saint Maximilian Kolbe—*priest and martyr in a Nazi concentration camp*
Mother Teresa of Calcutta—*apostle to the poor of India*
Dorothy Day—*apostle of peace and service to the poor*
Saint Frances Cabrini—*American citizen, worker among Italian immigrants*
Oscar Romero—*archbishop of San Salvador, martyred while celebrating Mass*
The Missionaries of El Salvador—*North American women martyred for helping the poor*

Our Catholic Tradition

Did you know that...

...we often pray without using words at all?

...kneeling is a sign of our humility before God?

...kneeling on one knee is called a genuflection?

...standing is a sign of alertness and readiness to listen?

...the sign of the cross demonstrates belief in the Trinity and the power of Jesus' death to save us?

...using holy water is a reminder of our baptism?

...a prayer repeated nine times is called a novena?

...many Catholics receive Communion on the First Friday of each month for nine months?

...fasting and abstinence are forms of prayer?

...fasting means eating only one full meal on a given day and just enough at two other meals to maintain strength?

...abstinence means refraining from eating meat?

...many American Catholics abstain every Friday as a prayer for world peace?

...fasting is practiced by most of the world's great religions?

...fasting helps clear our minds for prayer?

...folding one's hands is a sign of concentration in prayer?

...holding out one's hands palms upwards is a sign of our dependence on God?

...Christians once turned toward Jerusalem when they prayed?

...the rosary is an excellent form of prayer for those who feel deep anxiety?

...saying the rosary involves the body, recitation of words, use of the imagination, and prayers from the mind and heart?

...all the words said during the rosary come from either the Bible or very ancient traditions?

...sitting or kneeling quietly before the Blessed Sacrament is a prayer?

...some Catholics spend all night in prayer before the Blessed Sacrament?

...honoring Jesus in the Blessed Sacrament is the reason for a devotion called benediction?

...in benediction the consecrated host is placed in a holder called a monstrance so that all can see?

...incense is sometimes burned at liturgies and devotions to help people focus on their prayer?

...incense is a symbol of God's blessing enveloping the world?

Catholic Organizations

There are thousands of Catholic organizations of every imaginable kind. We have listed here only some of the more popular ones.

The Cursillo—a group of men and women who have made a special retreat and dedicated their lives to a pursuit of holiness through service to others.

Marriage Encounter—a program of retreats for married couples.

The Charismatic Movement—a loose-knit family of prayer groups who place great emphasis on informal, spontaneous prayer.

Small Christian Communities—local groups of people who meet regularly to discuss the Bible and its importance to the reality of their lives. These groups often send representatives to regional and diocesan leadership meetings.

The Knights of Columbus—a fraternal organization for Catholic men with special insurance options.

The Daughters of Isabella—a sorority for Catholic women.

Holy Childhood—a society to encourage children to support the missions.

The Legion of Mary—a spiritual community for men and women with emphasis on regular prayer, meetings, and service.

Third Orders—associations of men and women modeled after different religious communities with their own rules of life, meetings, and service projects.

C.Y.O.—Catholic Youth Organization, with emphasis on learning, recreation, prayer, and service to others.

National Council of Catholic Women (N.C.C.W.)—a confederation of many parish women's groups that holds diocesan and national meetings.

National Council of Catholic Men (N.C.C.M.)—a federation of men's groups that emphasizes formation of parish councils and diocesan renewal.

United States Conference of Catholic Bishops—the administrative wing of the American Bishops' Conference with offices and a large staff headquartered in Washington, D.C.

Apostleship of Prayer—an organization of Catholics devoted to the Sacred Heart of Jesus.

Cana Movement—small groups of married couples who work together to form local Christian communities.

Sodalities—groups of men and/or women searching for a richer spiritual life and marked by devotion to a particular saint, especially to Mary, the Mother of God.

Confraternities—groups of men and/or women dedicated to a special service or to some form of devotion.

Teens Encounter Christ—a program of retreats for youth.

St. Vincent de Paul Society—men and women who serve the poor through their parishes or citywide groups.

Catholic Worker Movement—men and women who set up and maintain houses of hospitality for the poor and live in community.

Serra Club—groups of Catholic laymen who promote church vocations.

The Teresians—Catholic laywomen's association with emphasis on prayer and service to others.

Holy Name Society—parish-based groups of Catholic men who receive Communion together.

Pax Christi—an international Catholic peace fellowship that works in the political arena for world peace.

Catholic Press Association—an association of publishers and editors of Catholic books, multimedia, and periodicals, especially those who work on diocesan newspapers.

National Catholic Education Association—an organization of Catholic school principals, teachers, and other educators.

The Newman Club—an organization of Catholic college students. Today many such organizations are called "campus ministry."

Campaign for Human Development—a program sponsored by the U.S. bishops to educate Catholics to the needs of the poor and to collect money for self-help projects.

Young Christian Students/Young Christian Workers—small groups of young people who study the gospels and attempt to implement them in the context of their daily lives.

National Catholic Rural Life Conference—an organization of Catholics devoted to the special concerns of rural people.

National Catholic Urban Coalition—organization of people concerned with the role of the church in urban settings.

The Sanctuary Movement—a loose organization of churches and synagogues which provide protection for illegal refugees.

Jesus Caritas—an international fraternity of priests.

Right to Life—a program concerned with abortion and other anti-life problems.

Religious Life

All Christians do not live out their commitment to Jesus in the same way. Those who want a celibate commitment and the community necessary to support it have always banded together for this special purpose.

History
In 313, after three centuries of persecution, the Emperor Constantine issued the Edict of Toleration which granted Christians the same rights as other citizens of the Roman Empire and later proclaimed Christianity the empire's official religion. Many believers were troubled by the spirit of wealth and luxury creeping into their churches and, to avoid being contaminated, left their ordinary lives and formed communities of sincere believers dedicated to prayer, fasting, and good works. This movement began in Egypt and quickly spread throughout the church. Within a hundred years or so, this monastic movement became more organized and usually included singing or reciting all or a part of a long series of daily prayers called the divine office, taking public vows, and wearing a distinctive uniform called a habit.

In the Catholic church today there are many such groups. Our tradition refers to them as "religious." All take public vows of poverty, chastity, and obedience, some other vows as well. They may or may not be priests. Their organization, the terms they use, and the styles of their lives depend largely on the era in which their group was founded.

Monks and Monasteries
For the first thousand years of Christianity, "religious" (men or women) left the "world" to form a kind of family whose main purpose was to sing the divine office and to live in community. They called their leaders abbots or abbesses and they called their homes monasteries, abbeys, or convents. A smaller monastery was a priory with a prior or prioress at its head.

Each monastery or abbey was an independent family, which made its own decisions and developed its own special lifestyle based on the talents of its members and the needs of the people around them. Monks were ordained priests only when the needs of the community or their neighbors demanded it. Today's Benedictines, Trappists, and Carmelite sisters maintain this lifestyle.

Friars and Convents
In early medieval times, the old forms of religious life were changed to fit new needs. The new religious no longer sang the office but did recite it, lived where people were, and put great emphasis on preaching. In the beginning most were not priests. The Dominicans and many groups of Franciscans maintain this tradition.

Sisters, Brothers, and the Poor
In early modern times, another new kind of religious community sprang up. Now religious might say only a part of the office, live where their work took them, and spend most of their time in charitable works like education, ministry to the poor, and, especially, missionary work. Their organizational model was an army and so their leaders were often called Mother General or Father General. Most modern communities of sisters and brothers and many groups of priests follow this tradition. Examples are the Jesuits, the Salesians, the Sisters of Charity, the Sisters of Mercy, and the Christian Brothers.

Modern Trends
All kinds of new religious communities are being tried today, some of which admit married people. It is too early to tell what these new religious communities will be like or what vocabulary they will use.

■ About the Church

Did you know that...

...there are over 1 billion Catholics in the world?

...over 60 million Americans are Catholic?

...Catholics live in every nation in the world, even in

places where they are routinely persecuted?

...there are 200 archdioceses and dioceses in the United States?

...there are over 19,000 parishes in the United States?

...there have been 264 popes, beginning with Saint Peter?

...there have been 37 anti-popes, men who claimed to be the pope but were rejected by the Church?

...the great question in the first-century church was whether Christians were obliged to obey the Jewish law?

...for the first three centuries Christians were routinely persecuted by Roman officials?

...the Roman Emperor Constantine established Christianity as the religion of the Empire in 313 A.D.?

...the first ecumenical council took place in 325 A.D. at a small town in present day Turkey called Nicaea?

...an ecumenical council is a meeting of all the world's bishops?

...it took centuries and six ecumenical councils for Christians to work out a formula that expressed their belief in the Trinity?

...in 1054 the churches of the East (Orthodox) separated from those ruled from Rome (Catholic)?

...one medieval European heresy, Albigensianism, forbade their members to marry?

...the church established the early European universities?

...philosophy and theology were the only reputable sciences in the Middle Ages?

...in the early 1400s three men claimed to be the legitimate pope? All had cardinals and bishops among their supporters.

...the ordained church leadership is called the hierarchy?

...a belief stated in words is called a doctrine?

...Martin Luther, leader of the Protestant Reformation, in the sixteenth century, did not set out to divide the church but to reform it from within?

...John Calvin, another leader of Protestantism, ruled Geneva as its religious and temporal lord?

...Henry VIII of England was once given the title "Defender of the Faith" by the pope and later excommunicated?

...the ecumenical council held in Trent, Italy attempted to reform the church in response to the Protestant Reformation?

...American Catholicism began with Spanish settlers in Florida and Georgia?

...the first English Catholics settled in Maryland?

...the first Catholic bishop in the United States was John Carroll whose cousin signed the Declaration of Independence?

...parochial schools are an American invention?

...many nineteenth-century American Catholics were involved in a heresy called "Trusteeism"?

...many American Catholic churches and convents were burned to the ground by rioting mobs in the nineteenth century?

...John F. Kennedy was the first Catholic to ever be elected president of the United States?

...Vatican II was the twentieth ecumenical council?

...Pope John XXIII hoped to reform the church and promote Christian unity by calling together the Second Vatican Council?

...The American bishops have written forward-looking pastoral letters on peace, the economy, and other major issues?

...In Latin America the official church has taken a "preferential option for the poor"?

...Some bishops and archbishops in the United States are African/American, Asian/American, or of Hispanic background?

A Matter of Rites

Not all Catholics worship God in the way most North American Catholics do. Catholics whose origin is in the Near East or Eastern Europe often have church customs very different from what we often think is the norm.

A group of Catholics who share the same spiritual heritage, have their own distinct theological system, practice their own type of monastic life, celebrate the Eucharist in their own way, and have their own ancient rules and regulations are called a "rite." Most, but not all, American Catholics are members of one rite, the Latin or Roman Rite.

Here is a list of the Rites recognized in the Catholic church today and the parts of the world where they are most common.

1. **Coptic**—very small group in Egypt
2. **Ethiopian**—tiny group limited to Ethiopia
3. **Syrian**—Middle East
4. **Malankar**—India
5. **Maronite**—Lebanon and the United States
6. **Greek**—Greece and surrounding areas, United States, and Canada
7. **Bulgarian**—Bulgaria
8. **Georgian**—Southern Russia
9. **Melchite**—Lebanon and United States
10. **Rumanian**—Romania
11. **Russian**—Russia and United States
12. **Serbian**—Yugoslavia
13. **Ukranian** or **Ruthenian**—parts of Russia and United States
14. **Belorussian**—Middle Europe
15. **Chaldean**—Middle East
16. **Malabar**—India
17. **Armenian**—Middle East
18. **Latin** or **Roman**—most parts of the world

Christianity Divided

Even though most Christians have sincerely tried to follow Jesus, they rarely have lived together serenely. Again and again, they have argued, fought, and even gone to war with one another over religious issues.

Here is a list of some of the most significant controversies. Those marked with an asterisk (*) are called "schisms," a term which indicates that no important doctrinal argument occurred. Those without the asterisk are called "heresies," a term that means that some matter of doctrine was involved in the dispute.

The Gnostic Controversy—A group of first- and second-century Christians attempted to synthesize Eastern religious thought and Christianity but were rejected by the church.

*The Easter Controversy—A struggle over the correct date of Easter raged in the church from the second until possibly the sixth century. Behind the scenes lurked a monumental struggle between local churches and the church in Rome. English and Irish Catholics were prominent in this controversy.

Arian Heresy—In the fourth century, theologians argued over the divinity of Jesus. Arians refused to accept the teaching of the Ecumenical Council of Nicaea that Jesus was both truly divine and truly human.

The Pelegian Heresy—Some Christians refused to believe that their own goodness was God's free gift. Some appear to have believed they could earn heaven by their own good works.

Iconoclasm—Some Christians did not accept use of images to foster devotion.

*East-West Schism—Churches of the Eastern Mediterranean and those in Western Europe divided. Today we refer to the East as the Orthodox churches and the West as the Catholic church.

The Albigensian Heresy—Manichaeism, which taught

that the human body and all material things were evil, fused with the Christian religion to form a bizarre sect known as the Albigensians.

*The Great Western Schism—At one time three different men claimed to be pope. Believers fought with one another over their claims.

Waldensian Heresy—The Waldensians were a group of French reformers who denied the importance of the sacraments and the necessity of the priesthood. They were the forerunners of Lutheranism and Calvinism.

The Lollards—a zealot group in England, which taught that the property of priests not in the state of grace might be confiscated.

Hussite Heresy—Christians who insisted that Holy Communion had to be distributed under the forms of bread and wine to be effective.

Lutheranism—originally a reform movement within Catholicism which later insisted that some Catholic practices were illegitimate.

Calvinism—a Swiss puritan movement that denied the importance of the sacraments and Roman authority. It later spread to other European lands. The majority of American Protestant churches trace their roots back to this movement.

Anglicanism—originally a schism in which the English church divided from the Roman church. Later, churchmen influenced by Calvinism took control and denied some traditional teachings.

Jansenism—a movement among some French Catholics which insisted that people's own perfections were enough to save them and demanded a very puritanical lifestyle. Although the group began in France, it had profound influence on Irish and, so, on United States Catholicism.

Methodism—began as a reform within the Anglican

church led by an Episcopal priest, John Wesley. Later it developed into a church of its own.

The Old Catholic Church—A group of Catholics who refused to accept the doctrine of papal infallibility and formed their own community.

Ecumenism

Christians on all sides of these ancient divisions today search for church unity. Theologians dialogue about the meaning of their various creeds. Church leaders work together to discover common approaches to contemporary problems. Laypeople of all denominations work and pray side by side. All these efforts toward Christian unity are called ecumenism. All major Christian churches support the movement.

Ordained Ministry

Anyone following Jesus in the Catholic church will discover a bewildering set of titles and offices, the result of 2,000 years of institutional life. Many of the questions these experiences suggest are related to ordination, one of the seven sacraments.

Q: Are all church workers ordained?
A: No. Most people who work in the church are not ordained. For example, no women including religious sisters are ordained and ordination to most church offices is reserved to celibate males.

Q: Who is ordained?
A: Five kinds of ministers are ordained: bishops, priests, deacons, acolytes, and lectors. However, both men and women may serve as lectors and altar servers though they are not ordained.

Q: Are all bishops heads of dioceses?
A: In theory, they are since they are ordained to serve in specific places. In practice, many are ordained to serve in dioceses that

no longer exist except on paper and spend their lives as assistants to other bishops or working in important church offices.

Q: Are all priests pastors?
A: Not at all. Priests may serve the church in almost any way. Some are teachers, others are administrators, and many serve as assistants to pastors.

Q: May all priests lead the community in Mass?
A: Yes, they may unless church authorities have forbidden them. Priests who have left the active ministry are forbidden to lead the Eucharist although they were once ordained to do so and their ordination is understood to be permanent.

Q: What do deacons do?
A: Deacons are ordained to serve the church in a variety of ways including preaching, baptizing, distributing Communion, and other liturgical functions.

Q: May deacons marry?
A: Married men may be ordained deacons but should their wives die they may not remarry.

Q: Why does the church refuse married people ordination?
A: Church authorities insist that they must have the total commitment of their ordained ministers and a marriage would interfere with this commitment. The church accepts married deacons but rarely as full-time church employees. Today many Catholics want this church rule changed and insist on rethinking this old custom.

Faith and Community

The Catholic church calls itself a community of faith. In it both individuals and groups find a home as they seek to follow Jesus.

Faith is a deeply personal affair in which an individual forms an intense relationship with Jesus. Whether we first learn about Jesus by living in the faith community and observing others or discover him on our own makes little difference. We must form a personal relationship with him.

Yet, it is difficult to sustain such a relationship without the help of other people who also have that kind of relationship with the Lord. We naturally gather together to support and strengthen one another in our resolve to follow Jesus. This gathering together is community. Thus, the community is born of personal faith and has as its goal supporting the faith conviction of its members.

We can and must study and be aware of the ways this community has organized itself under the guidance of the Holy Spirit. However, the organization is not the community and no amount of knowledge about the church can save us. Only Jesus saves.

To foster the community life of the church, many have become religious sisters, brothers and priests, or joined lay confraternities and movements. Each age seems to have had its own way of building community. In our day, devoted Christians are forming small groups who study, pray and work together. These groups are often called small ecclesial communities or the little churches of the everyday believers. The movement began in South America and is rapidly influencing people in our own lands as well.

The Church and Mission

Following Jesus means much more than praying and leading a decent life. Every Catholic is called to share the good news with those near and far. Catholics have a long history of evangelizing others by preaching and serving others, especially the poor.

The words apostle and missionary come from the same ancient Arabic word. Apostle is taken from the Greek and missionary from the Latin translations. Christians have always known that Jesus wanted them to share the good news of his resurrection and triumph over death and sin with all of God's children wherever they might live.

Today the Catholic church thinks of itself as truly missionary. Here are some of the words theologians use when talking about this aspect of the church's life:

Mission—the task Jesus gave the church to teach all nations what he had taught them.

Missionary—men and women who take on this task as their profession.

Lay Missionaries—men and women who are neither priests or religious but who are professional missionaries.

Foreign Missions—missionary projects that are outside the land the missionaries come from.

Home Missions—missionary projects that are located in the same country the missionaries are from.

Mission Sending Societies—groups of men and women, usually religious or priests, who recruit, train, send, and supervise missionaries in foreign lands.

Reverse Mission—the experience many missionaries have of learning many things about Jesus from the people they serve. Some organizations have been set up to take well-to-do North Americans to poorer lands to learn about God from the poor.

Medical Missions—programs of sharing the love of Jesus through good medical care.

Educational Missions—programs of sharing the love of Jesus by setting up schools and educating young people to take their place in society. Catholic schools in the United States and Canada are outstanding examples of this kind of mission.

Evangelization—another word for sharing the good news.

Missiology—the systematic study of missionary experiences and ideals.

Focus on the Sacraments & Public Prayer

Catholic Christians celebrate what they believe about following Jesus. They do this both as individuals and as a community of faith. Official public celebrations include the seven sacramental rituals and the divine office. Unofficial public worship includes many kinds of devotions that change as the needs of people change. This section of *Basics of the Catholic Faith* shares with you some of the key ideas and trends in Catholic worship.

The Seven Sacraments

Those who follow Jesus believe they are never alone. Jesus, his Father, the Spirit and the community of faith are ever with those who believe. There are seven sacred signs of God's presence in the lives of believers which we call sacraments.

Sacraments of Christian Initiation *These three sacraments immerse a person in the church, the Body of Christ.*	**Baptism** **Confirmation** **Eucharist**
Sacraments of Healing *These two sacraments offer Christ's healing touch of forgiveness and peace.*	**Penance (Reconciliation)** **Anointing of the Sick**
Sacraments of Mission *These sacraments are expressions of the call of every baptized Christian to follow Christ in a particular way.*	**Holy Orders** **Matrimony**

About the Sacraments

Did you know that...

...it took the church several centuries to sort out the number of sacraments?

...not all Christians today believe in seven sacraments?

...the Council of Trent (1543–1563) defined the traditional Christian belief in seven sacraments?

...all sacraments involve the whole community?

...the church itself is sometimes called the "eighth sacrament"?

...Baptism welcomes a person into the Christian community?

...records of infant Baptism go back to the earliest days?

...at one time people postponed Baptism until the end of their lives?

...Baptism is necessary to receive any other sacrament?

...Baptism can be given in three ways: by immersing the whole body in water, by pouring water over the head, or by sprinkling water on the head?

...going into the water is a symbol of death to old ways, dying with Christ?

...some theologians taught that unbaptized infants did not go to heaven but to a special place they called limbo?

...limbo is a theological opinion, not official church doctrine?

...Baptism today often takes place during Sunday Mass?

...parents, not godparents, are central in today's infant baptismal liturgy?

...Catholics do not ordinarily rebaptize converts from other Christian denominations?

...Baptism, Confirmation, and Holy Orders can be received only once?

...in Eastern churches and among many Spanish-speaking peoples, Confirmation is administered at Baptism?

...in some Protestant churches, Confirmation must be administered before Eucharist is received?

...in some Catholic parishes, Confirmation is not administered until adulthood?

...Holy Orders has three grades, unlike any other sacrament?

...the church ordains married men in some countries and everywhere under special circumstances?

...in the past, young boys were ordained?

...bishops, priests, and deacons all receive the Sacrament of Holy Orders?

...many Catholic theologians see no biblical or theological reason why women cannot be ordained priests and deacons?

...the Sacrament of Penance is also called Reconciliation?

...confession of sin is part of the Sacrament of Penance?

...at one time, Penance was received only once in a person's life?

...Penance was once reserved for three sins: idolatry, adultery, and murder?

...Reconciliation once required years of fasting and penance?

...people wishing to be reconciled to the church once wore special clothing and begged prayers at the entrance to the church?

...church law once forbade private confession of sin?

...the Sacrament of Penance can be received together in a group ceremony?

...requiring a priest and two other witnesses at a marriage is a rather recent church law?

...under some circumstances the church recognizes common-law marriages?

...divorce was rather commonly practiced in the church for nearly a thousand years?

...Christians were once forbidden to remarry after the death of their spouse?

...the church discourages marriage with those who do not believe in Jesus and even with other Christians who are not Catholic?

...Jesus is really present in the Eucharist?

...one receives the body and blood of Christ under the form of bread or wine?

...the first part of the Mass is based on the old synagogue service?

...those not baptized and those baptized but not in good standing were once forbidden to remain in the church for the liturgy of the Lord's Supper?

...in some Eastern liturgies, the Eucharistic Prayer takes place behind a screen, hidden from the people?

...Latin is still the official language of the liturgy and may always be used?

...some Catholics have refused to accept the new liturgy of Vatican II?

...Catholics use unleavened bread but most Eastern churches insist on leavened bread for Eucharist?

...Anointing of the Sick used to be called Extreme Unction?

...any Catholic who is sick may receive Anointing of the Sick?

...anointing sometimes brings about bodily cures?

Examination of Conscience

Jesus said that no one could serve both God and money (Matthew 6:24). Avoiding the net that greed has spun around our wealthy society is difficult. Yet, it is the basis of any sincere Christian lifestyle.

How would you answer the following questions?

1. Do you think new is better than old?

2. Do you eat more than you need?

3. Do you buy expensive foods to impress others?

4. Are you often discontented with your clothing?

5. Do you buy expensive clothes to impress others?

6. Do you desire or already own an expensive car?

7. Do you buy expensive gadgets?

8. What does your home say about your values?

9. Would you rather make something or buy something?

10. Do you buy things because you are bored or feeling unfulfilled?

11. Do you give time and money to the poor?

12. Do you share with others without complaint?

Our attitude toward riches is often our most fundamental moral value. It influences the way we act toward other groups of people, toward the poor, toward other nations, and toward ourselves. Our society is based on acquisition, our religion on renunciation and simplicity of life.

■ About Reconciliation

As Christians we believe that baptism brings a person to a whole new life. We speak of this new life in many different ways, for example, being "sinless" and "pleasing to God." We believe that the newly baptized person is as innocent as a newborn baby. When we Christians slip into a life of sin and are cut off from the community of believers, we are invited to reform our lives, and begin anew to follow Christ. We do this in the sacrament of Penance or reconciliation. This sacrament includes both the confession of our sins and reconciliation with God and community.

During medieval times, people sought reconciliation in private from monks, and so the custom of private confession was born. Today we confess our sins to God in the presence of a priest who represents the community. He then reconciles us in the community's name. It is God who forgives sin, of course, but it is the community of faith that announces that reconciliation in God's name.

The Rite of Penance
After the Second Vatican Council the Rite of Penance was changed to reflect the communal nature of both sin and reconciliation. This sacrament may be celebrated in different ways. It may be a one-on-one encounter between a penitent and his confessor, a group celebration in which each peni-

tent confesses his or her sins and receives absolution individually or in very special cases the whole group may make a general confession of their sin and together receive absolution. The ways we prepare for the sacrament and receive it are very similar. Following is an outline of this Rite:

Introduction—Priest and penitent spend a short time focusing on God's loving forgiveness. This is more elaborate for groups than for individuals. For individuals a few words may suffice while hymns and formal prayers may be necessary to help a group attain the same focus.

Celebration of the Word—One or more readings from the Bible help us remember God's loving kindness. One of these readings is always from the gospels.

Reconciliation—Except in unusual circumstances, each person confesses his or her personal sin, prays for God's forgiveness and then receives a suggested penance from the priest. The priest then repeats the words of absolution, an outward sign that God has indeed forgiven us.

Conclusion—Once again priest and penitent spend a few moments thanking God for his mercy. For groups this will naturally be more elaborate than for individuals.

Sacramental Symbols

Water—purification

Immersion in water—
death to sin

Salt—faith

Oil—strength

Light—Christian life

Rings—unity and endless love

Laying on of hands—
transfer of power
and healing

Embrace—
unity among believers

Bread and wine—
signs of Christ's presence

Other Symbols

Christian art and liturgy are rich in symbols. Here are a few you will see often:

Liturgical Colors

White—purity and joy

Purple/Dark blue—sorrow for sin, penitence

Red—courage, love, dedication

Green—hope, peace

Black (no longer used)—death

Gold—the fullness of joy

Other Common Symbols

Trumpet—judgment day

Anchor—hope

Acadia bush—immortality

Cedar tree—strength

Evergreen tree—immortality

Fig tree—fruitfulness

Oak tree—strength

Olive tree or branches—peace

Palm branches—joy

Symbols of the Trinity
God the Father, Jesus, the son of God, and the Holy Spirit.

The triangle—Trinity of God

Wheat sheaves—bounty of God

Six-pointed star—God, the Creator

Eye—wisdom and knowledge of God

Dove—Spirit of God

Symbols of Jesus

Lamb—suffering servant of the Lord

Crucifix—death of Jesus

Jeweled cross— the resurrection

Jesus Candle—Christ, the light of the world

Vine and its branches— Jesus, the center of unity among all people

Sun—Jesus, light of the world, source of warmth and power

Crown—Jesus triumphant over death

Heart—Jesus as pure love

Phoenix—Jesus risen from the dead

Pelican—Jesus feeding his children with his own blood

Butterfly—Jesus risen

Alpha and Omega— Jesus the beginning and end of all

INRI—abbreviation for Jesus of Nazareth, King of the Jews

IHS—Greek abbreviation for Jesus

Fish—Greek letters stand for Jesus Christ, Son of God, Savior

Chi Rho—Greek abbreviation for Christ

The Four Evangelists

Man sometimes winged—Matthew

Lion—Mark

Ox sometimes winged— Luke

Eagle—John

Church Authority

Bishop's staff or crozier

Tiara or papal crown

Bishop's hat or miter

Keys crossed

Chasuble (outer garment of priests and bishops)

Stole (worn over both shoulders of a priest or bishop and over one shoulder of a deacon)

The Divine Office

All monks must sing the office in common each day. Many other religious are also obliged to recite it together. All priests must also say the office, whether in private or with others. Office comes from the Latin word meaning "duty" and the divine office is the church's duty to God.

The office is divided into parts to be sung at different times during the day. The traditional parts are:

Matins—a long three-part office to be sung during the night before the sun comes up

Lauds—the official morning prayer to be said around sunrise

Prime—a prayer before starting the working day

Terce—a prayer for mid-morning

Sext—a noonday prayer

None—a mid-afternoon prayer

Vespers—evening prayer for late afternoon or early evening

Compline—night prayer before going to bed.

Today's liturgical reforms allow many simplifications in the old format, but a basic structure of prayer before daybreak, morning and evening prayer remains essential to the church's obligation to praise the Lord from the rising of the sun to its going down.

The Order of the Mass

The rites and actions of the Mass are modeled on the family gathering for meals. The family members set the table (the preparation), say grace (the Eucharistic Prayer), and share the food (Communion).

The Introductory Rites
(the gathering)

Greeting

Penitential rite

Kyrie ("Lord, have mercy")

Gloria (in season)

Opening prayer

The Liturgy of the Word

First reading

Responsorial psalm

Second reading

Alleluia

Gospel reading

Homily

Creed

General intercessions

The Liturgy of the Eucharist

Preparation of the gifts
>   The presentation of the gifts
>
>   Preparation of the bread and wine

Prayer over the gifts
>   The Eucharistic Prayer
>
>   Preface
>
>   Acclamation (Holy, holy, holy Lord)
>
>   Eucharistic Prayer

Communion Rite
>   The Lord's Prayer
>
>   The breaking of the bread
>
>   Holy Communion
>
>   The prayer after Communion

The Concluding Rite
(dismissal)

Greeting

Blessing

Dismissal

The Church Year

The church organizes its focus of prayer and celebration of the sacraments around two great mysteries: the birth of Jesus and his resurrection from the dead. Just as these are the two most important dogmas of faith so they are the center of liturgical prayer. What we believe always directs the way in which we pray.

The Christmas Cycle

Preparation: Advent is a time for remembering the first coming of Jesus and meditating on the importance of his final coming. Advent begins on the fourth Sunday before December 25th and continues through Christmas Eve. It is a time for special prayer and fasting.

Celebration: Christmas Day begins the celebration which continues through the week after Epiphany celebrated on January 6th—the day for exchanging gifts in many lands. In the United States the Epiphany is celebrated on the Sunday nearest the traditional date.

Remembering: A quiet time of the year that follows and continues until the beginning of Lent. We call this ordinary time.

The Easter Cycle

Preparation: Lent begins forty days before Easter with the celebration of Ash Wednesday and becomes more intense in its final two weeks called Passion Time. The last week of Lent is called Holy Week and Thursday, Friday, and Saturday of that week are especially important days of preparation for Easter. Adult baptism ordinarily takes place during the Easter Vigil when all Catholics are invited to renew their own baptismal promises.

Celebration: Easter Day begins the celebration of Jesus' resurrection from the dead which continues for seven weeks until the week of Pentecost Sunday, the day on which the Holy Spirit descended on the first believers. The Ascension of the Lord is celebrated during this time.

Remembering: The quiet period of the year is resumed and lasts until Advent is ready to begin once more.

Special Days

All through the year, days are set aside to remember important events in the life of Jesus (e.g., the Ascension), Mary (e.g. the Immaculate Conception) and the saints (e.g., Saint Patrick's Day). In medieval times, war was forbidden on many of these days and peasants had the right to remain home from work. The holy days are such a part of our culture that we still celebrate many of them. Our word *holiday* is an obvious development from *holy day*.

Theological Words

Over the centuries theologians have pondered the depths of meaning they discovered in the sacraments. Like all specialists they have used words that often mystify the casual observer. Here are some of those words that can help you deepen your own understanding of the sacraments.

Valid—real and effective

Ex opere operato—sacraments do not depend on the holiness of those who administer them

Matter—the essential thing used in the ritual (e.g., water in Baptism) forms the essential words for the sacrament

Character—the effect of Baptism, Confirmation, and Holy Orders which makes loss of these sacraments impossible

Res et sacramentum—the effect of all sacraments that remains after the ritual is over

Transubstantiation—a way of expressing the reality of Jesus' presence in Eucharist in philosophical terms

State of grace—condition of being in God's favor as opposed to being cut off from God by deliberate serious sin

Mortal sin—sin that destroys the life of God within us

Venial sin—less serious sin that does not completely break our relationship with God

Infused virtues—divine help given with the sacraments, which makes it easier to do good and avoid evil

Acquired virtues—good habits that are acquired by repetitive action

Liturgy—public worship of the church

Divine office—a series of daily prayers sung or recited by priests and many religious and by some laypeople

Conversion—personal acceptance of faith, also called "quickening" and "Baptism of the Holy Spirit" by other Christians

Indissolubility—quality of permanence in marriage. Another way of saying "Marriage is forever."

Focus on Devotions

Christianity is always anchored in what we can know of Jesus' life in the first century and in the lives of his followers through the centuries since then. People in each century and in various cultures have found different ways to unite with Jesus. We call these ways *devotions* to distinguish them for the public liturgy of the church which is for all cultures and all ages.

Devotions wax and wane as cultures change. Looking over the centuries since Jesus' death and resurrection can give us a deeper understanding of the ways our ancestors thought about Jesus and at times can uncover a devotion that is just right for us at this moment of our lives.

Devotions to Jesus

Through the centuries since Jesus' death and resurrection, saints and mystics have imagined him in many different ways, ways that made it easier for them to pray.

Here are a few of the ways Christians of our past have thought about and prayed to Jesus.

Christ the King—Jesus is pictured as ruler of the universe who leads the way to God's kingdom. He taught through word and example that service to others is the way to this kingdom.

The Sacred Heart—Pictures of Jesus show his wounded heart exposed with a crown of thorns entwined about it. This devotion stresses the compassion and love Jesus has for all humankind and the suffering that love caused him.

The Precious Blood—Among ancient people, blood was a symbol of life. Death came when the blood was poured out. This devotion calls attention to the price Jesus paid for his compassion toward humanity.

The Holy Name of Jesus—The name of a person answers the question, who are you. Devotion to the name of Jesus is to his unique personality which united both the human and divine.

The Good Shepherd—This is an image Jesus himself used to describe his role of caring for all his people. Such devotion stresses the tenderness and compassion of the Lord.

The Eucharistic Jesus—Catholics believe that Jesus is present in the appearances of bread and wine in the Eucharist. This devotion encourages frequent reception of Holy Communion and prayer before the Blessed Sacrament.

The Holy Cross—Devotion to the suffering Jesus in his last agony is very popular among Catholics. The heroism of Jesus under pain and his compassion for others is evident in this devotion.

Jesus, the Worker—Although official church policy discourages identifying Jesus with any class of people, many focus on the simple life Jesus led and his closeness to the oppressed and poor of the world.

Jesus, the Prophet—Jesus can easily be pictured as the Father's spokesperson, the one who brings his message to the world. This devotion stresses the determined courage of Jesus in the face of powerful opposition.

The Priestly Jesus—Jesus is sometimes pictured in priestly robes offering himself as a sacrifice. He is both the priest who offers the sacrifice and the victim.

Mary

Catholics have a special fondness for Mary, the mother of Jesus. That devotion is anchored in the teachings of the ancient church. It was the Council of Ephesus in 431 which declared that Mary was indeed the "Mother of God."

Some of the feast days and titles of Mary are:

The Mother of God—January 1st

Our Lady of Lourdes—February 11th

The Annunciation—March 25th

The Visitation—May 31st

The Immaculate Heart of Mary—a Saturday in June

The Assumption—August 15th

Birth of Mary—September 8th

Our Lady of Sorrows—September 15th

Presentation of Mary—November 21st

The Immaculate Conception—December 8th

Our Lady of Guadalupe—December 12th

Mary's role is also celebrated in many of the great feasts of Jesus since she was so intimately involved with him in all aspects of his life.

Catholics ask Mary, as they ask all the saints, to join her prayers with theirs in praise, thanksgiving and petition. What better way to pray than in solidarity with the mother of God?

The Rosary

One of many Catholics' favorite prayers is the rosary. In it they find an opportunity to revisit many important moments in the lives of Jesus and Mary.

History

No one is sure exactly when the rosary began although it was probably some time during the Middle Ages. Many unlettered people attended the chanting of the office in the monasteries and listened reverently to the monks as they sang psalm after psalm. These people often had a great devotion to Mary and knew the Lord's Prayer, the Hail Mary, and the Doxology (Glory be to the Father...) by heart. The stage was set for organizing these repetitious prayers just as the monks had already organized their own prayer.

Slowly the custom arose of reciting the Hail Mary 150 times since there were 150 psalms. Keeping count was difficult so the 150 were divided into tens which could be easily counted on one's fingers and a Lord's Prayer was added at the beginning and end of each decade while the Doxology was used to end it.

People soon began to use pieces of knotted string to help them keep count. With time these counters were made more elaborate and prayers were added at the beginning and end of the decades. Most people did not recite all fifteen decades each day but were content with five. Thus, our rosaries today have five decades on them.

Meditation

The rosary was never meant to be a mindless repetition of empty words. People had always thought about God and talked to him in their hearts as they said the prayers. The church slowly evolved fifteen scenes taken from the Bible to match the fifteen decades. They were the recommended subjects for meditation and are often announced when the rosary is said in public. They are usually called the mysteries of the rosary.

These mysteries are divided into three sets of five. The first recalls joyful events in the early life of Jesus, the second, sorrowful moments during his passion, and the third, times of glory after his resurrection.

The Fifteen Mysteries

The Joyful Mysteries
(usually remembered on Monday and Thursday)

1. The Annunciation to Mary that she was to be the mother of Jesus
2. The Visitation by Mary to her cousin Elizabeth
3. The Birth of Jesus in Bethlehem
4. The Presentation of Jesus in the Temple by Joseph and Mary
5. The Finding of Jesus in the Temple at twelve years of age

The Sorrowful Mysteries
(usually remembered on Tuesday and Friday)

1. The Agony in the Garden of Olives
2. The Scourging at the Pillar
3. The Crowning of Jesus with Thorns

4. The Stripping of Jesus' Garments

5. The Crucifixion and Death of Jesus

The Glorious Mysteries
(usually remembered on Sunday, Wednesday, and Saturday)

1. The Resurrection of Jesus from the Dead

2. The Ascension of Jesus into Heaven

3. The Coming of the Holy Spirit on Pentecost

4. The Assumption of Mary into Heaven

5. The Coronation of Mary, Queen of All the Saints

Beginning and Ending

Before saying the five decades, people usually say the Apostles' Creed, a Lord's Prayer, three Hail Marys, and a Doxology. At the end of the prayer, they usually add the Hail Holy Queen prayer.

Angels

From ancient Judaism, Christians inherited a belief in spirits created by God before the beginning of the world. Most Catholics have treasured this belief.

In Greek the word angel means "messenger" for one task of these spirits was to bring messages to humans from the Lord. Both the Old and New Testaments mention angels including three by name: Michael, Gabriel, and Raphael.

Medieval theologians, after searching the Bible for names of angels, taught there were nine choirs of these spirits:

1. archangels
2. angels
3. cherubim
4. seraphim
5. virtues
6. powers
7. principalities
8. thrones
9. dominions

Many also taught that God assigned to each person and institution a guardian angel.

Because angels are friends of God, believers have always asked them to join their prayers of praise, petition, and thanksgiving. The church liturgy remembers angels several times each year. Artists picture angels as human beings with wings or as tiny, playful infants.

The Saints

In the Apostles' Creed all Christians profess a belief in the "communion of saints," the unity that exists among all who believe, whether they are living or dead.

Believers have long singled out men and women of outstanding commitment to Jesus for special honor. For centuries, local communities and their bishops decided who was worthy of that honor and of the title "saint." In medieval times, a strict investigation became necessary before anyone could be honored as a saint.

Today Catholics rely on a special Vatican congregation to make these investigations. At the end of their first investigation, they declare that a person practiced heroic virtue. We call that person "venerable." A second investigation results in the title "blessed." The third and final investigation brings the title "saint."

Catholics have never confined their devotion to these canonized saints. Most families honor members who were exceptionally holy. Many people who died only recently are regarded as saints long before they are canonized by church officials.

Catholics do not hesitate to invite the saints to pray to the Lord with them. They believe that these men and women are close to God and care about their brothers and sisters who are still struggling to live out their commitment to the Lord.

A list of some of the more popular saints begins on page 48.

Pictures, Icons, and Statues

As soon as Christians had gathering places of their own in which to worship, they decorated them with pictures, bas-reliefs, icons, and statues. Works of art reminded them of Jesus, Mary, the apostles, and the early martyrs.

Art was an unselfconscious act of remembrance and praise. We find such religious art in the Roman catacombs and in the earliest churches. Naturally, Christians did not worship the works of art but what they represented. From time to time, fundamentalist zealots have tried to forbid the use of all images by Christians. Good sense has always won out, however, and today every medium and every art form, from stained glass to marble and from abstract painting to banner and poster realism, adorn Christian churches and homes. We need art to help us pray just as we need pictures of our loved ones who have died to keep their memory alive among us.

Shrines, Processions, and Pilgrimages

Like to visit special places that help you remember important people and events? Christians have always made their journeys to the Holy Land and to other significant locations.

Believers called the places they visited shrines and their trips pilgrimages. In medieval times, historians tell us that as many as one in twenty Europeans were on pilgrimage at a single time. Catholics still make their pilgrimages and visit special shrines.

This century has rediscovered the emotional solidarity of

marching for a purpose. Catholics have long practiced marching in what the liturgy calls processions in honor of Jesus, Mary, or one of the saints. Sometimes our processions contain themes from our traditional piety and in protest against existing social evils.

Marching in honor of Jesus in the Blessed Sacrament is the most popular of these processions and is practiced around the feast of Corpus Christi (Body of Christ) in early June. Another popular procession is one held in many areas during May to honor Mary, the mother of Jesus.

Prayer for the Dead

Living or dead, all believers are bound together into a union so close that Saint Paul says we make up the one body of Christ.

Because we are so united, we routinely pray for one another. Mothers pray for their children and children for their parents. We support one another in prayer.

Our prayers for the dead are no different. We pray for those who have gone before us that they may enjoy eternal life. The church has long taught that what is evil in our lives when we die must be purged out so that we can enjoy being with God forever. Our prayers for the dead support them during that process of preparation we call purgatory. We hope that others will, in turn, support us when we come to that period of our lives.

Focus on Lifestyle

As Catholic Christians we are called to live out the gospel in our daily lives, and this includes obedience to the ten commandments. In John's gospel Jesus declared, "This is my commandment: love one another as I have loved you." As times change, as our life changes and as we develop, the demands of gospel living will take different forms. Underlying it all, however, is Jesus' desire that we love one another. In this section of *Basics of the Catholic Faith* are guidelines and insights from Christians who have tried to live the gospel message.

Our Creed

What we believe is the cornerstone of the way we live. Here is a simple statement of what Catholics believe and how they hope to act.

We have been made in God's image and likeness and we have been adopted as God's own children. Jesus is our brother. We are Mary's children and one with all the saints who have done God's will throughout the ages.

We are unique reflections of God, people so special that we have never been seen before and will never be seen again. God so treasures us that if it had been necessary Jesus would have died on the cross for us alone. As it is, God touched our souls in baptism and in confirmation strengthened all our powers. More than once, God has forgiven us and invited us to share in the body and blood of Jesus.

Because we are so special, we have no need to pile up riches in order to impress others, to manipulate other people, to be disloyal or untrue, to be selfish and self-centered, or to practice injustice of any kind. We are free to follow our best instincts and act like the children of God, members of God's beloved family.

Christian Lifestyle

Jesus spoke clearly about the lifestyle he expected from his followers in the following passage from the gospel of Matthew.

When the Son of Man comes in his glory, and all the angels with him...all the nations will be gathered before him, and he will separate people one from another as a shepherd separates the sheep from the goats, and he will put the sheep at his right hand and the goats at the left. Then the king will say to those at his right hand, "Come, you that are blessed by my Father, inherit the kingdom prepared for you from the foundation of the world; for I was hungry and you gave me food, I was thirsty and you gave me something to drink, I was a stranger and you welcomed me, I was naked and you gave me clothing, I was sick and you took care of me, I was in prison and you visited me." Then the righteous will answer him, "Lord, when was it that we saw you hungry and gave you food, or thirsty and gave you something to drink? And when was it that we saw you a stranger and welcomed you, or naked and gave you clothing? And when was it that we saw you sick or in prison and visited you?" And the king will answer them, "Truly I tell you, just as you did it to one of the least of these who are members of my family, you did it to me."

MATTHEW 25:31–40

Standing With the Poor

Human history is always changing. As it does it demands different kinds of dedication from the followers of Jesus.

After the Second Vatican Council, bishops from Latin America used the words "preferential option for the poor" to explain the church's need to side with the poor in their struggle for justice. They invited all Christians to make a preferential option for the poor. Choosing this option has cost the church dearly. Priests have been killed, bishops vilified and murdered, sisters tortured to death, and men and women catechists killed by the thousands. Today's church, like the church of the early centuries, is a church of martyrs, men and women giving witness to the truth that without justice Christianity is ever incomplete.

We live in an age of martyrs—men and women, priests, sisters, brothers, lay missioners and catechists, witnessing to their preferential option for the poor. All Catholic Christians are called to live the same faith.

Mother Teresa of Calcutta put it this way:

Just allow people to see Jesus in you,
to see how you pray,
to see how you lead a pure life,
to see how you deal with your family,
to see how much peace there is in your family.
Then you can look straight into their eyes
and say, "This is the way." You speak from life.
You speak from experience.

The Two Ways

According to two very different thinkers, Sigmund Freud and Ignatius of Loyola, each human life must point in one of two directions.

1. The first direction is *inward (toward self)*. If you have this direction, you worry about what others think, strive to be rich, powerful, and prestigious so that you will feel successful. Your relationships with others are important only to the degree that they make you feel good about yourself. You compete with other people and find it difficult to let anyone get ahead of you.

2. The second direction is *outward (toward others)*. If you have this direction to your life, you think about other people and their feelings. You tend to forget yourself and serve the needs of others. You enjoy cooperating and rarely compete. You treasure relationships not because they make you feel good but because they are helpful to other people.

The Ten Commandments

From the desert days of Israel, believers understood that they had a responsibility to live as children of God. They attempted to codify some of their most important duties in what we call the Ten Commandments.

1. I am the Lord your God. You shall not have strange gods before me.
2. You shall not take the name of the Lord your God in vain.
3. Remember to keep the Lord's day holy.
4. Honor your mother and your father.
5. You shall not kill.
6. You shall not commit adultery.
7. You shall not steal.
8. You shall not bear false witness against your neighbor.
9. You shall not covet your neighbor's wife.
10. You shall not covet your neighbor's goods

The Two Great Commandments

When asked what was the greatest commandment Jesus replied:

1. You shall love the Lord your God with all your heart, and with all your soul, and with all your strength, and with all your mind,

2. and love your neighbor as yourself.

LUKE 10:27

The Gift of Love

In his letter to the Christians at Corinth, St. Paul spoke of a "way that surpasses all others." Jesus commanded his followers to love one another and here Paul describes what such love means.

Love is patient; love is kind; love is not envious or boastful or arrogant or rude. It does not insist on its own way; it is not irritable or resentful; it does not rejoice in wrongdoing, but rejoices in the truth. It bears all things, believes all things, hopes all things, endures all things. Love never ends. But as for prophecies, they will come to an end; as for tongues, they will cease; as for knowledge, it will come to an end. For we know only in part, and we prophesy only in part; but when the complete comes, the partial will come to an end. When I was a child, I spoke like a child, I thought like a child, I reasoned like a child; when I became an adult, I put an end to childish ways. For now we see in a mirror, dimly, but then we will see face to face. Now I know only in part; then I will know fully, even as I have been fully known. And now faith, hope, and love abide, these three; and the greatest of these is love.   1 CORINTHIANS 13:4-13

The Beatitudes

The moral teaching of Jesus is summed up in this short passage from Saint Matthew's gospel. All who claim to follow Jesus must take these simple statements seriously and integrate Jesus' lofty ideals into their everyday life.

Blessed are the poor in spirit, for theirs is the kingdom of heaven.

Blessed are the meek, for they will inherit the earth.

Blessed are those who mourn, for they will be comforted.

Blessed are those who hunger and thirst for righteousness, for they will be filled.

Blessed are the merciful, for they will receive mercy.

Blessed are the pure in heart, for they will see God.

Blessed are the peacemakers, for they will be called children of God.

Blessed are those who are persecuted for righteousness' sake, for theirs is the kingdom of heaven.

Blessed are you when people revile you and persecute you and utter all kinds of evil against you falsely on my account. Rejoice and be glad, for your reward is great in heaven, for in the same way they persecuted the prophets who were before you.

Signs of the Holy Spirit

Through the centuries, theologians and mystics have pondered the Bible for clues of the working of the Holy Spirit in the lives of believers. They have listed nineteen virtues or qualities that are inspired by the Spirit of God. Some we call "gifts" and others we call "fruits" of the Spirit dwelling in a cooperative heart. When we recognize these qualities in our own lives we can be sure the Holy Spirit is at work in us.

Gifts of the Holy Spirit

wisdom	fortitude	piety
understanding	knowledge	fear of the Lord
counsel		

(These gifts were first mentioned in Isaiah.)

Fruits of the Holy Spirit

charity	benignity	faith
joy	goodness	modesty
peace	long-suffering	continence
patience	mildness	chastity

(These virtues are listed in Saint Paul's letter to the Galatians.)

The Cardinal Virtues

Theologians have identified the four central human virtues on which a holy life hinges. They are called "cardinal" since the original meaning of this word in Latin is "hinge." These virtues are:

Prudence   Justice   Fortitude   Temperance

The Capital Sins

Just as theologians list virtues, so they also list sins. Some vices are more significant than others because they are what motivate us to sin. They reflect an attitude of selfishness, of concern for oneself at the expense of others. They are called "capital" sins because they are at the heart of all sin.

Pride   Covetousness   Lust   Anger

Gluttony   Envy   Sloth

The Works of Mercy

Following Jesus means imitating the way he related to others. Medieval theologians listed fourteen essential signs that one is indeed acting toward others the way Jesus did.

The Corporal Works of Mercy

1. To feed the hungry.

2. To give drink to the thirsty.

3. To clothe the naked.

4. To visit the imprisoned.

5. To shelter the homeless.

6. To visit the sick.

7. To bury the dead.

The Spiritual Works of Mercy

1. To admonish the sinner.

2. To instruct the ignorant.

3. To counsel the doubtful.

4. To comfort the sorrowful.

5. To bear wrongs patiently.

6. To forgive all injuries.

7. To pray for the living and the dead.

Church Commandments

All communities have their rules and the Catholic church is no exception. It has a large volume of law called "canon law," a huge body of work that deals with the structures and administration of the church as well as with sacraments and spirituality. Most Catholics, however, seldom come into contact with canon law. There are, however, six important rules that do affect everyday Catholic life. They are called the commandments of the church.

1. To attend Mass on Sundays and holy days of obligation.

2. To fast and abstain on the days appointed.

3. To confess our sins at least once a year.

4. To receive Holy Communion during Eastertime.

5. To contribute to the support of the church.

6. To observe the laws of the church concerning marriage.

Stages of Growth

Often psychologists can help us understand our struggles to follow Jesus. Psychology, like all science, searches for truth. When it finds the truth it can often help us in our journey toward God.

Erik Erikson, an influential twentieth-century psychologist, noted these eight challenges to growth that all humans encounter. Ordinarily one must be completed before the next challenge can be undertaken. Failure to master these challenges results in the conditions indicated in parentheses.

1. Trust (mistrust): The challenge of the infant years is to have confidence in the provider.

2. Autonomy (shame or doubt): The challenge of pre-school years is to become independent while still trusting.

3. Initiative (guilt): The challenge of the early school years is to begin to assume responsibility for one's own actions.

4. Industry (inferiority): The challenge of the junior high and early high school years is to initiate and complete activities on one's own and overcome exploitation by others.

5. Identity (role confusion): The challenge of the late adolescent years is to accept and love one's inner self.

6. Intimacy (isolation): The challenge of the young adult years is to discover a partner or a reference group, which will support further growth.

7. Generativity (stagnation): The challenge of middle life is to assume responsibility for the next generation.

8. Integrity (despair): The challenge of the mature years is to achieve wisdom, leadership, and self-confidence.

Many religious educators and pastoral leaders find this schema helpful in identifying the needs of their people and use it as a basis of program planning and counseling. Many individuals find it helpful in understanding their own challenges.

Stages of Moral Development

Lawrence Kohlberg, a Harvard researcher, theorized that there are six distinct motives that we all use to make our decisions. He also noted that we pass from one motive to another as we become older and wiser with the years. Many people stop at any one of these stages of growth and for whatever reason refuse to advance to a more mature understanding of good and evil. According to Kohlberg, once we have moved to a higher stage we can never return to a lower one even if we try to. His research can help us understand our own struggles in deciding our life's direction.

These are the six stages he identified:

Stage One: My moral decisions are no more than accepting the judgment of some person in power. My primary motivation is to avoid being punished by the person in authority. Children often say, "If I do that, I will get in trouble."

Stage Two: My moral decisions now are mine rather than someone else's but they are self-centered. My primary motivation is to be sure that my own emotional and physical needs are met. Anything that keeps me from my own satisfaction is wrong. Children often say, "That's not fair" but mean "I am not getting my due."

Stage Three: My moral decisions are now based on a desire to be accepted by another individual. My primary motivation is to be accepted by one other person. Anything that destroys my relationship with that person is evil. Children and many adults often never go beyond this stage in which morality has no fixed principles.

Stage Four: My moral decisions are now based on a desire to be accepted not by an individual but by the culture, an institution such as a government or a church. I often couch my moral decisions as duty. My primary motivation is to be a "good citizen" or a "good church member," to be respectable. Most people never go beyond this stage.

Stage Five: My moral judgments are now based on principles that the culture, the institution, may or may not accept. I am now able to say, "This is right or this is wrong even when I am alone in my judgment." I will try to influence others and the institutions I love to accept a deeper understanding of morality.

Stage Six: My moral judgments are now based on my own conscience and I attempt to apply all moral judgments with consistency and profound respect for others. Few ever achieve this level.

Human Rights

*Pope John XXIII summed up traditional Catholic teaching on human rights in his 1963 encyclical letter, **Peace on Earth**. Because every person has these basic rights, all other people and all governments are obliged to respect and provide for them. Catholics should be concerned with the rights of all people, especially the poor and powerless.*

These are the basic human rights Pope John listed:

The right to:
- life
- bodily integrity
- food
- clothing
- shelter
- rest
- medical care

- social services and security...
    in cases of sickness
    inability to work
    widowhood
    old age
    unemployment
- respect
- a good reputation
- freedom in searching for the truth...
    in expressing and communicating opinions in pursuit of art
- be informed truthfully about public events
- a share in the benefits of culture
- basic education
- technical and professional training
- honor God and practice religion
- choose freely a state in life
- set up a family with equal rights and duties for men and women
- safe and healthy working conditions
- a just wage
- private property
- form associations
- immigrate and emigrate
- take an active part in the political process
- enjoy protection of all rights under law.

These human rights form the basis of all Catholic social teaching. Popes, ecumenical councils, conferences of bishops, individual bishops, priests, theologians, and teachers all try to apply these principles to the everyday problems of our world.

Global Problems

Catholic leaders regularly apply the teachings of Jesus and the experience of living the Christian life for some twenty centuries to modern problems. Here are three such statements:

World Hunger

The right to have a share of earthly goods sufficient for oneself and one's family belongs to everyone. The Fathers and Doctors of the Church held this view, teaching that all are obliged to come to the relief of the poor, and to do so not merely out of their superfluous goods. If a person is in extreme necessity, he has the right to take from the riches of others what he himself needs. Since there are so many people in the world afflicted by hunger, this (Second Vatican) Council urges all, both individuals and governments, to remember the saying of the Fathers: "Feed the man dying of hunger, because if you have not fed him you have killed him."

CONSTITUTION ON THE CHURCH IN THE MODERN WORLD (#69)

World Peace

At the center of the church's teaching on peace and at the center of all Catholic social teaching are the transcendence of God and the dignity of the human person. The human person is the clearest reflection of God's presence in the world; all of the church's work in pursuit of both justice and peace is designed to protect and promote the dignity of every person. For each person not only reflects God, but also is the expression of God's creative work and the meaning of Christ's redemptive ministry. Christians approach the problem of war and peace with fear and reverence. God is the Lord of life, and so each human life is sacred; modern warfare threatens the obliteration of human life on a previously unimaginable scale. The sense of awe and "fear of the

Lord" which former generations felt in approaching these issues weighs upon us with new urgency. In the words of the pastoral constitution: "Men of this generation should realize that they will have to render an account of their warlike behavior; the destiny of generations to come depends largely on the decisions they make today."

U.S. CATHOLIC BISHOPS

The Economy

We write to share our teaching, to raise questions, to challenge one another to live our faith in the world. We write as heirs of the biblical prophets who summon us "to do justice, to love kindness and to walk humbly with our God" (Micah 6:8); and we write as followers of Jesus, who told us in the Sermon on the Mount: "Blessed are the poor in spirit...Blessed are the lowly...Blessed are those who hunger and thirst for justice...You are the salt of the earth...You are the light of the world" (Matthew 5:1-6, 13-14). These words challenge us not only as believers, but also as consumers, citizens, workers and owners. In the Parable of the Last Judgment Jesus said, "I was hungry and you gave me to eat, thirsty and you gave me to drink...As often as you did it for one of these the least of my brothers, you did it for me" (Matthew 2:35-40). The challenge for us is to discover in our own place and time what it means to be "poor in spirit" and the "salt of the earth" and what it means "to serve the least among us" and "to hunger and thirst for justice."

U.S. CATHOLIC BISHOPS

Significant Lifestyle Guides

Here are a few of the many guidelines for following Christ from contemporary Christians as well as Christians throughout the ages.

Riches are like those who hold them tightly; they not only hinder one but pierce and wound. How many rich people of our day are clad with material dyed with the sweat and blood of the poor because the clothes they wear are woven out of theft, larceny, usury, and illegitimate gain?

SAINT ANTHONY

No longer do we take the sword against other nations, nor do we learn war anymore since we have become the sons of peace through Jesus.   ORIGEN IN THE 3RD CENTURY

The spirit is truly the dwelling of the saints and the saints are for the spirit a place where he dwells as his own home.

SAINT BASIL

It is possible to offer fervent prayer even while walking in public or strolling alone, or seated in your workplace…while buying or selling…or even while cooking.

SAINT JOHN CHRYSOSTOM

For me prayer is a surge of the heart; it is a simple look turned toward heaven, it is a cry of recognition and of love, embracing both trial and joy.   SAINT THÉRÈSE OF LISIEUX

There is only one unhappiness and this is not to be one of the saints.   LEON BLOY

Make ready for the Christ, whose smile like lightning sets free the song of everlasting glory that now sleeps in your paper flesh like dynamite.   THOMAS MERTON

The "community of God" is a community in which the power structures prevailing in the world are broken down. All are equal, though we might say that the lowly, the poor, and the oppressed are more equal than others are.

EDWARD SCHILLEBEECKX, THEOLOGIAN

When Jesus is with us all is well and nothing seems difficult; but when Jesus is absent everything in life is hard and distasteful.   THOMAS À KEMPIS

No one has the right to sit down and feel hopeless. There's too much work to do.   DOROTHY DAY

I would not make it through the struggle if I were not a believer. I had more than one very comfortable proposition offered to me by the government. I did not accept them because I preferred to struggle for my cause.   LECH WALESA

Whatever the program, for whatever purpose or cause, if love is not there, then beware. Without love, there can be temporary successes but in time they crumble.

POPE JOHN XXIII

Focus on Private Prayer

What is done in the great public prayers of the church must begin quietly within the hearts of individual women and men. Not even the greatest of liturgies can replace the sincerity and eager searching of hearts turned toward God. In this section of *Basics of the Catholic Faith* are some favorite prayers of Catholics.

Why We Pray

Since medieval times theologians have identified four reasons why we humans pray to God, our loving Father. They are:

1. To praise him for his goodness just as we spontaneously compliment others who are good and kind.

2. To thank him for his many gifts to us including the life we live, the food we eat, and the people who love us.

3. To ask him for favors since all good things come from him and we depend completely on his goodness.

4. To ask for his forgiveness since we, like all human beings, are sinners and often neglect our duties to him and to our neighbor.

Ways to Pray

Prayer exists on different levels just as our conversations may be more or less intense. At the most intense level, words are unnecessary. The three major expressions of the life of prayer recognized and encouraged by our tradition are vocal prayer, meditation, and contemplative prayer.

Favorite Prayers

A Morning Prayer

In the name of the Father and of the Son and of the Holy Spirit, may I begin this day. May God be with me in all its moments, and watch over me until another night has come. Amen.

A Prayer of Praise ("Gloria")

Glory to God in the highest, and peace to his people on earth.

Lord God, heavenly King, almighty God and Father,

We worship you, we give you thanks, we praise you for your glory.

Lord Jesus Christ, only Son of the Father, Lord God, Lamb of God,

You take away the sin of the world: have mercy on us;

You are seated at the right hand of the Father: receive our prayer.

For you alone are the Holy One, you alone are the Lord,

You alone are the Most High, Jesus Christ, with the Holy Spirit,

In the glory of God the Father. Amen.

A Prayer for Faith, Hope, and Love

I believe, O Lord; may I believe yet more firmly.

I trust in you, O Lord; may I trust you yet more firmly.

I love you, O Lord; may I love you yet more deeply.

Guide me by your wisdom.

Keep me in your justice.

Comfort me by your mercy.

Protect me by your power.

Make me prudent with my neighbor,

steadfast in all dangers,

patient in my trials,

humble in my successes,

and joyful in all things.

Psalm 100

Make a joyful noise to the LORD, all the earth.
Worship the LORD with gladness;
come into his presence with singing.

Know that the LORD is God.
It is he that made us, and we are his;
we are his people, and the sheep of his pasture.

Enter his gates with thanksgiving,
and his courts with praise.
Give thanks to him, bless his name.

For the LORD is good;
his steadfast love endures forever,
and his faithfulness to all generations.

The Hail Mary

Hail, Mary, full of grace, the Lord is with you!
Blessed are you among women,
and blessed is the fruit of your womb, Jesus.
Holy Mary, Mother of God,
pray for us sinners, now and at the hour of our death.
Amen.

The Doxology

Glory to the Father,
  and to the Son,
  and to the Holy Spirit:
  as it was in the beginning,
  is now,
  and will be forever. Amen.

A Daily Offering

Jesus, through your mother Mary,

I offer you all my prayers, deeds, joys, and sufferings
  of this day,

In union with the prayers of all good Christian
  people everywhere.

I pray for the intentions of your Sacred Heart.

Grant our world peace and our families love,
  and grant joy to people everywhere.

Amen.

The Magnificat (Mary's Prayer)

My soul magnifies the Lord,
    and my spirit rejoices in God my Savior,
for you have looked with favor on the lowliness
    of your servant.
Surely, from now on all generations will call me blessed;
    for you, Mighty One, have done great things for me,
    and holy is your name.
Your mercy is for those who fear you from generation
    to generation.
    You have shown strength with your arm;
    you have scattered the proud
    in the thoughts of their hearts.
You have brought down the powerful from their thrones,
    and lifted up the lowly;
You have filled the hungry with good things,
    and sent the rich away empty.
You have helped your servant Israel,
    in remembrance of your mercy,
    according to the promise you made to our ancestors,
    to Abraham and to his descendants forever.

LUKE 1:46–55

The Lord's Prayer

Our Father, who art in heaven,
hallowed be thy name:
thy kingdom come;
thy will be done on earth as it is in heaven.
Give us this day our daily bread;
and forgive us our trespasses
as we forgive those who trespass against us;
and lead us not into temptation,
but deliver us from evil.
For thine is the kingdom and the power and the glory, forever.
Amen.

The Apostles' Creed

I believe in God, the Father almighty,
    creator of heaven and earth.
I believe in Jesus Christ, his only Son, our Lord.
    He was conceived by the power of the Holy Spirit
    and born of the Virgin Mary.
    He suffered under Pontius Pilate,
    was crucified, died, and was buried.
    He descended to the dead.
    On the third day he rose again.
    He ascended into heaven,
    and is seated at the right hand of the Father.
    He will come again to judge the living and the dead.
I believe in the Holy Spirit,
    the holy catholic church,
    the communion of saints,
    the forgiveness of sins,
    the resurrection of the body,
    and life everlasting.

Psalm 57

My heart is steadfast, O God,
 my heart is steadfast.
I will sing and make melody.
Awake, my soul!
Awake, O harp and lyre!
I will awake the dawn.

I will give thanks to you, O Lord, among the peoples;
 will sing praises to you among the nations.
For your steadfast love is as high as the heavens;
 your faithfulness extends to the clouds.
Be exalted, O God, above the heavens.
 Let your glory be over all the earth.

Prayer for the Spirit of God

Come, Holy Spirit, fill the hearts of your faithful
 and kindle in them the fire of your love.
Send forth your Spirit, and they shall be re-created;
 and you will renew the face of the earth.

An Examination of the Day

Spend a few minutes rejoicing over the good things in your day and expressing sorrow over the thoughts, words, and actions that you now see as selfish and unworthy. Here are some questions to stimulate your reflection:

My life with God

Do I think of God during the day and talk to him in my own words?

Do I make a sincere effort to participate in Mass?

Do I have confidence in God in the midst of daily troubles?

Do others respect God and love him because of my example?

Is God real in my life, a close friend, someone with whom I feel comfortable?

My life within myself

Do I accept being the person I am realizing I am the very best of God's creation?

Do I treat myself with respect and reverence?

Have I mistreated my own body, God's temple, by misusing drugs or alcohol?

Am I developing the talents God gave me?

Do I let discouragement overpower me and become morose or depressed?

Have I excused myself from guilt because "everyone is doing it"?

Am I trying to make friends with others? With God?

My life with others

Am I honestly able to say I love my neighbor as myself?

Do I love those close to me, in my family, at work, at school?

Do I try to dominate others?

Do I try to monopolize others, fearing their love for others somehow diminishes their love for me?

Do I willingly share what I have with others?

Do I argue over money?

Am I honest with others, willing to appear in a bad light rather than lie to them?

Am I respectful of others? Of the poor? Of other races? Of those who do not agree with me?

Do I associate only with those whose friendship might be helpful to me?

Do I lose my temper often?

Do I talk too much about myself and fail to listen to what others have to say?

Do I take what belongs to others?

Do I cheat?

Am I understanding of the faults of others?

Do I gossip?

Am I willing to speak out against injustice wherever I see it?

Do I help the poor and downtrodden?

Do I make little of others' experience and intelligence?

An Act of Joy and Sorrow

O my good God,
  I thank you for the joys of this day—
  for the gift of life itself,
    for family and friends,
    for all good things
  which come to me from your creative hand.
  I am sorry for my daily sins—
  for selfishness and thoughtlessness,
  for all that is mean and miserly,
  for neglect of your many children
    whom you have called on me to love.
  Direct tomorrow's steps in your path
  and give me the peace of knowing I am always
    with you.
  Amen.

The Jesus Prayer

Lord Jesus Christ,
Son of the Living God,
have mercy on me, a sinner.

A Prayer to Mary

Remember, O most gracious Virgin Mary, that never was it known that anyone who fled to your protection, implored your help, or sought your intercession, was left unaided. Inspired by this confidence, I fly to you, O Virgin of Virgins, my Mother. To you I come, before you I stand, sinful and sorrowful. O Mother of the Word Incarnate, despise not my petitions, but in your mercy hear and answer me. Amen.

A Prayer for the Church

Remember, Lord, your holy church.

Deliver us from all evil

Make us perfect in your love.

Gather us from the four corners of the earth,

and make us holy men and women.

For the kingdom, the power, and the glory are yours

now and forever. Amen.

A Prayer for Blessing

May he support us all the day long, till the shadows length-en and the evening comes, and the busy world is hushed, and the fever of life is over and our work is done. Then in his mercy may he give us a safe lodging, a holy rest and peace at last. Amen.   CARDINAL NEWMAN

Lord God, we can hope for others nothing better than the happiness we desire for ourselves. Therefore, I pray to you, separate me not after death from those I have tenderly loved on earth. Grant, I pray you, that where I am, they may be with me and that I may enjoy their presence in heaven after being so often deprived of it on earth. Lord, God, I ask you to receive your beloved children straightway into your life-giving heart. After their brief life on earth, give them eternal happiness.   SAINT AMBROSE

A Searcher's Prayer

Gracious and holy Father,
give us the wisdom to discover you,
     the intelligence to understand you,
     the diligence to seek after you,
     the patience to wait for you,
     eyes to behold you,
     a heart to meditate on you,
     and a life to proclaim you,
     through the power of the Spirit of Jesus, our Lord.
     Amen.   SAINT BENEDICT

A Prayer for Courage

Give me whatever you ask of me,
    then ask of me whatever you will, Lord.
Remember that we are only dust,
    for of the dust you have made us!
But I can do anything
    in him who strengthens me;
Lord, strengthen me, and I can do everything!
Give me whatever you ask of me,
    then ask of me what you will.
Amen.   SAINT AUGUSTINE

Union With Jesus

Christ be with me.
Christ be before me.
Christ be behind me.
Christ within me.
Christ beneath me.
Christ above me.
Christ at my right hand
    and at my left.
Christ in the heart of everyone who thinks of me.
Christ in the mouth of everyone who speaks to me.
Christ in every eye that sees me.
Christ in every ear that hears me.
                                    SAINT PATRICK

A Prayer for Peace

Lord, make me an instrument of your peace:
    where there is hatred, let me sow love;
    where there is injury, pardon;
    where there is doubt, faith;
    where there is despair, hope;
    where there is darkness, light;
    and where there is sadness, joy.
O Divine Master, grant that I may not seek so much
    to be consoled as to console,
    to be understood as to understand,
    to be loved as to love.
For it is in giving that we receive,
    it is in pardoning that we are pardoned,
    and it is in dying that we are born to eternal life.

SAINT FRANCIS OF ASSISI

Day by Day

Thank you, Lord Jesus Christ,
    for all the benefits and blessings
    which you have given me,
    for all the pains and insults
    which you have borne for me.
Merciful Friend, Brother and Redeemer,
    may I know you more clearly,
    love you more dearly,
    and follow you more nearly day by day.

SAINT RICHARD OF CHICHESTER

For Insight

May the Lord Jesus touch our eyes,
    then we shall begin to see in visible things
    those which are invisible.
May he open our eyes to gaze,
    not on present realities,
    but on the blessings to come.
May he open the eyes of our heart
    to contemplate God in Spirit,
through Jesus Christ the Lord,
    to whom belong power and glory
    through all eternity.
Amen.   ORIGEN

For a Holy Heart

Lord, grant me a holy heart
    that sees always what is fine and pure
    and is not frightened at the sight of sin,
    but creates order wherever it goes.
Grant me a heart that knows nothing
    of boredom, weeping, and sighing.
Let me not be too concerned
    with the bothersome thing
    I call myself.
Lord, give me a sense of humor
    and I will find happiness in life
    and profit for others.
                SAINT THOMAS MORE

Index

National Catholic Rural Life
  Conference, 55
National Catholic Urban
  Coalition, 55
Nazareth, 1,3,11,23,75
New Testament, 28-30
Newman Club, 55
Nicene Creed, 5,6,10
Noah, 33

Office, Divine, 56,67,76,80
Old Testament, 26-28
Order of the Mass, 77
Origen, 106,125
Orthodox, 58,61

Palestine, 14,18,19,27,33,35,36
Parables of Jesus, 21-22
Parish Council, 45,47
Parish Societies, 45,47
Pastor, 45,46
Patmos, 13
Pax Christi, 54
Peace, 33,42,47,51,52,59,68,74,94,
  97,104-105,124
Penance, 46,70,72,73
Pentateuch, 26,32
Person, 10-11
Pilgrimages, 23,88
Pope, 42-43
Prayer, reasons for, 110
Prayers, 109-125

Preferential Option, 59,93
Priests, 43-44,56,57,63,70,75,76,
  80,93,103
Prior, Prioress, 56
Processions, 88-89
Prophets, 25,28,34,37,105
Protestantism, 59
Provincial, 45

Q Document, 14

Reconciliation, 46,70,72-73
Religious Orders, 43,44-45
Reverse Mission, 66
Right to Life, 55
Rites, 60
Rosary, 46,52,84-86
Ruth, 36

Sacraments, 67-80
Saints, 48-51
  Ambrose, 48,122
  Anselm, 49
  Anthony, 48,106
  Augustine, 48,123
  Barnabas, 34
  Benedict, 49,122
  Francis of Assisi, 49,124
  Ignatius of Loyola, 50,94
  James, 30,34
  Patrick, 48,123
  Paul, 29,35,48

Of Related Interest...

Catholic Customs & Traditions
A Popular Guide
Greg Dues

From Candlemas to the Easter candle, the rosary, meal prayers, the Christmas tree, Easter eggs, and much more, Dues traces the vast riches of the traditions, customs, and ritual practices that make up the Roman Catholic experience. He discusses the nature of religious traditions; the temporal cycle with its rich variety of customs; the Catholic tradition of honoring Mary and the saints; and more. An invaluable, thorough reference book.   224 pages, $9.95 (order C-14)

Faith Alive
A New Presentation of Catholic Belief and Practice
Rowanne Pasco and John Redford, General Editors

A lively, up-to-date, and complete presentation of Catholicism, incorporating key references to the Bible, the teachings of Vatican Council II, prayers, and other important sources of Catholic teaching. Includes questions for discussion, a comprehensive index, and a listing of common Catholic prayers. An indispensable book on contemporary Catholic belief and practice.   312 pages, $12.95 (order C-22)

While You Were Gone
*A Handbook for Returning Catholics *And Those Thinking About It*
William J. Bausch

An overview of the changes that have taken place in the church since Vatican II, presented in a non-threatening and welcoming manner. A very popular book with pastors and leaders.   112 pp, $5.95 (order B-91)

This Is Our Mass
Tom Coyle

In down-to-earth language the author presents the basic elements of liturgy and the historical, liturgical, and spiritual dimensions of the Mass. Through example and story he links the celebration of the Eucharist to daily life. Chapters include: "To Worship Is to Love," "What's in a Church?" and "God Speaks to Us."
160 pages, $7.95 (order B-78)

Available at religious bookstores or from:

TWENTY-THIRD PUBLICATIONS
A Division of Bayard PO BOX 180 • MYSTIC, CT 06355
1-800-321-0411 • FAX: 1-800-572-0788 • E-MAIL: ttpubs@aol.com
www.twentythirdpublications.com
Call for a free catalog